ETHICS IN THE PRESENCE OF CHRIST

ETHICS IN THE PRESENCE OF CHRIST

CHRISTOPHER R. J. HOLMES

t & t clark

Published by T&T Clark International
A Continuum Imprint
The Tower Building, 11 York Road, London SE1 7NX
80 Maiden Lane, Suite 704, New York, NY 10038

www.continuumbooks.com

British Library Cataloguing-in-Publication Data
A catalogue record for this book is available from the British Library

ISBN: 978-0-567-14428-7 (hardback)
       978-0-567-49173-2 (paperback)

Typeset by Fakenham Prepress Solutions, Fakenham, Norfolk NR21 8NN
Printed and bound in India

CONTENTS

PREFACE

In the Anglican tradition, after the Old Testament and the Epistle are read, the reader announces, 'This is the Word of the Lord', to which the people of God respond, 'Thanks be to God'. My work as a preacher and an academic theologian is an attempt continually to inhabit this Word and so to help others to the end that the triune God of the Gospel's name be hallowed and praised. This Word is, I believe, a very present Word, a Word that is near to 'you, on your lips and in your heart' (Rom. 10.8). But to hear the Bible as God's address to God's people, indeed God's world, is difficult for many to do, given that we have created a world which functions without any recourse to the living God. This book is the fruit of a few years worth of reflection on Scripture *as* the Word of the Lord, in particular Scripture as presenting to us a Lord who is present, and as present ministering. It is a work in moral ontology which argues that the Gospel gives us a God who claims women and men for his service with a view to the world's humanization.

I consider it a great privilege to help students and congregants hear Scripture as denoting an event that is radically formative and world-constituting. One of the great joys of preaching and teaching Christian doctrine is to help others better see that doctrines describe, albeit often but through a glass darkly, what is real and going on. Doctrine, when it yields to the incarnate Word as attested by the written and so proclaimed Word, does not simply describe a rather domesticated state of affairs wherein Christians simply recite what has always been believed to be the case. Instead, description of doctrine is a far more apocalyptically charged affair: to think after, indeed to follow after and to map what the God of Israel has done, is doing, and will do in Jesus Christ by the power of the Spirit so as to enable humanity to participate in the fullness of the promises of the covenant: 'You will be my people' (Ezek. 37.27).

To the extent that this text helps students, ministers, and other academic theologians and ethicists to hear Scripture as denoting a present and so ministering Word, it will have succeeded. Christology is indeed concerned with the basic question 'Who is Jesus Christ?' and ethics the question, 'What is he doing?' Jesus Christ's enactment of his identity, as narratively attested, radically implicates. Ethics is but human activity beholden to his presence as One who continually gathers through his Word and by his Spirit women and men to himself, upholding and sending them into his world as his witnesses to his glorified life. Jesus Christ is the light of the world. The present tense matters, and so Christians, I argue, are but those formed by and those rendered participant in his light that continually shines in the darkness.

I would not have been able to write this book without many conversations with postgraduate students at Providence Theological Seminary (Manitoba, Canada) and now at the University of Otago (New Zealand). In particular, I would like to thank the students of my Christian Ethics class at Providence Seminary and the many able Otago postgraduates in Systematic Theology who have helped me to see better the moral force of the present tense concerning Christ's person. My debts also extend to individual theologians who have responded to the manuscript in various phases of its development, first in Canada and more recently in New Zealand. They are: Tim Perry, John Webster, Paul Molnar, Philip Ziegler, Nancy Duff, Joe Mangina, Christopher Morse, Rachel Muers, and Murray Rae. My genuine thanks also go out to my colleague Paul Trebilco for his close reading of the final draft of the manuscript and to Mark Gingerich, now completing his doctorate at Otago, for copy-editing, production of the index, and the making of extremely helpful suggestions as to the final shape of the argument.

Last, I owe an enormous debt of gratitude to my *Doktorvater* David Demson, Professor of Systematic Theology Emeritus at Emmanuel College, University of Toronto and now of Wycliffe College, University of Toronto. David's humour, warmth and interest in my family and me over the last several years have not gone unnoticed. He was a superb director and continues to be a trusted friend and most incisive theologian. It is to him that I dedicate this book with thanksgiving.

Christopher R. J. Holmes
Lent, 2011

Chapter 1

ETHICS AND PRESENCE

In this essay I present a descriptive account of the presence and ongoing ministry of Jesus Christ, specifically the character of his power, truth and love, and the import of this power, truth and love for ethics.[1] A focus on the presence of Christ is one that is uncommon in contemporary offerings in ethics. One might hear much about the church but at times rather little about Christ's person and what it is that he is now doing. And so, I want to talk about ethics in light of the contemporary presence and ministry of Jesus, to sketch an account of ethics from the side of Jesus Christ. I take seriously that ethics is a function of an account of Jesus Christ, the human counterpart to Christ's obedience of faith. Ethics is simply action evoked by and participant in his saving action and saving obedience. Accordingly, ethics is behavior that recognizes 'the pioneer and perfecter' of our faith.[2] Ethics involves taking up the Christological foundation of ethics, the sense in which Christ is ethics' pioneer, but also the fact that ethics is a function of Christ's 'continually operative' reconciling and revealing intervention, his perfecting work.[3] As a matter of acts

---

[1] Of course there are other attributes – or better, perfections – peculiar to the person of Jesus Christ, e.g., holiness, mercy, justice, etc., which *could* very well be the focus of this essay. However, I focus on these three because I would very much like to extend in a more Christologically concentrated fashion the work of Wolf Krötke, whose important monograph *Gottes Klarheiten* treats God's truth, love, power and eternity as *clarifying* of human life. See further Wolf Krötke, *Gottes Klarheiten: Eine Neuinterpretation der Lehre von Gottes 'Eigenschaften'* (Tübingen: Mohr Siebeck, 2001). See also Christopher R. J. Holmes, 'God's Attributes as God's Clarities: Wolf Krötke's Doctrine of the Divine Attributes', *International Journal of Systematic Theology* 10 (January 2008): 54–72. Note that all translations of Krötke's work are my own.

[2] See Heb. 12.2.

[3] Thomas F. Torrance, *Atonement: The Person and Work of Christ*, ed. Robert T. Walker (Downers Grove, IL: IVP Academic, 2009), 70.

1

not only grounded in Christ but sustained by him, ethics is, if it be Christian, where Christ begins and ends, reigning supreme, eliciting human action transparent to his presence and action.

The purpose of this essay is to show the many ways in which the presence of Christ's power, truth and love create a strange new world.[4] What is strange and new is that the presence of Christ's power, truth and love tells us something about what *is*. There is a place for an account of reality – for ontology – in Christian ethics. This essay unfolds the *is*, the new situation, the new world, which *is* as a result of Christ's saving activity. This essay also unfolds the imperative that follows from the 'is', the way in which the 'is' is being brought into being by Christ himself. The indicative, you might say, is generative and inclusive of an imperative. The divine side of ethics is generative of the human side, and the human side, while human, is as such because reality – the divine side – wills to be actualized in us. By locating ethics first and foremost on the divine side, the human side is not for this reason compromised: the human side is as a result of the divine side.

When the Christian community attends to the presence and ministry of the person into which it has been incorporated, the pioneer and perfecter of its faith, it discovers that it has a great deal of learning to do with respect to the character of his power, truth and love. What it begins to learn above all else is that the power, truth and love of Christ, as they are present to the Christian community and to the world in his person, *define* the space in which the community and the individual Christian act. There is a corollary, however: lest one fear that there will be a 'like it or lump it' mentality at work in this essay, the aim is to read Jesus' history, as narratively attested at crucial points in John's Gospel, as giving us a purchase on the real world that is coming to be.[5] The nature of reality matters, if human action indeed be ethical, but not reality understood in a static sense. Reality is dynamic: it is simply what God in Christ is doing by the power of the Spirit to make all things new.[6]

---

[4] 'Strange' and 'new' is of course a reference to Barth's famous essay 'The Strange New World within the Bible', in *The Word of God and the Word of Man*, trans. Douglas Horton (Cleveland, OH: Pilgrim Press, 1928).

[5] See *Dietrich Bonhoeffer Works*, ed. Wayne Whitson Floyd Jr., vol. 8, *Letters and Papers from Prison*, ed. John W. de Gruchy (Minneapolis: Fortress Press, 2010), 373 (hereafter cited as *DBW*). This is Bonhoeffer's (in)famous 'criticism' of Barth's so-called 'positivism of revelation'.

[6] See Rev. 21.5.

I have chosen to work with John's Gospel because it, of all the Gospels, is most transparent in its identification of Jesus as divine, as the basis, establishment and perfection of reality. Jesus as narratively attested is, for John, very much present in the mode of the Spirit as the One he is. In a manner clearly different from the Synoptics, but not in opposition to them, John's portrait elides, because of the promised *paraclete*, any sense in which Jesus' ministry can be considered to be 'back there'. Jesus continues to be present and, as present, ministers through his Word and by the power of his Holy Spirit. Jesus is – John would have us believe – *the* truth of God and who we are in light of God's making himself known in the One who is the light of life. To be sure, it is not as if these emphases are not present to varying degrees in other biblical books. Rather, it is the case that for the apostolic mind as evinced by John, it is inconceivable to set forth Christ as One who does not, in the promised Spirit, continue to make himself known. All the moments of Jesus' life, his death, his resurrection and his ascension, reveal God's glory. 'Truly to see him is to see who God is'.[7] To think about ethics Christianly, that is in light of reality, is to think within the sphere of God's glory, God's propensity for giving of himself to the creature. That is what this essay seeks to do: to gloss the exalted Christology of the Fourth Gospel with a view to offering an account of ethics that understands itself to be the human response to the question 'What is Jesus now doing?' The exaltation and glorification of the crucified Jesus is a matter of the here and now. Again, this is not to suggest that Paul, for example, would argue otherwise. Rather, it is simply to attend to one portrait in a way that is sensitive to its uniqueness as concerns its presentation of Jesus' ministry and its culmination on the cross as, in the power of the Spirit, possessing a revelatory and so claiming character.

The Christian tradition has recognized at certain key junctions that talk about what Jesus Christ does can never be isolated from who Jesus Christ *is*. There is thus no ontological distinction between the *person* and the *work* of Christ: the eternal person of the Son is reiterated in what the Jew Jesus does. However, following Bonhoeffer, an account of Christ's person has priority with respect to an account of his work: 'When I know *who* he is, who does this, I will know *what* it is he does'.[8] Ethics benefits from sustained inquiry into the who,

---

[7] D. Moody Smith, *The Theology of the Gospel of John* (Cambridge: Cambridge University Press, 1995), 133.

[8] Dietrich Bonhoeffer, *Christ the Center*, trans. Edwin H. Robertson (San Francisco: HarperCollins, 1978), 39.

for only when the who is established can we know what it is that he
is doing, and what it is that we are to do. Doing is, you might say, a
function of who we are in him. His person has contemporary force
such that his ministry becomes through the Spirit active in us.

This is an essay about the person of Christ as that which not only
grounds but generates ethics, and by ethics I mean neither principles
for living nor a set of rules that are valid in all times and places for
all people. What I do mean, instead, is a description of what kinds of
human acts the individual and the church ought to undertake, so as
to be most transparent to the saving Gospel that lies at its centre and
to which it is continually being summoned and conformed. Ethics is
not, then, a matter of conformity to so-called moral principles, but is
rather about being a form of life 'oriented toward revelation'.[9] Herein
lies the eschatological or apocalyptic moment at the essay's heart.
Ethical acts are acts aligned to the presence of a particular person,
and to what he is now doing. Accordingly, ethics is not concerned with
the good abstractly understood or indeed with any norm or concept
apart from a particular *living* person. Christians must continually turn
to *the* person who speaks through his Word, a Word which must be
heard in season and out of season. In so doing, they are transformed
into his image and thereby, through feeding upon him at his Table by
faith with thanksgiving, made new. 'Jesus Christ, the perfect human
image of God because the perfect divine image, brings human life in
himself back to its perfect beginning – the perfect beginning that in a
sense never was – so that it might be achieved in a way not susceptible
of loss'.[10]

The essay asks and answers two basic questions: Is this One as
narratively attested present? And if so, what is he doing? When ethics
becomes attuned to how God's rule in the world takes shape through
the present Christ and how God intends his rule to take shape in us
through patient hearing of the Word, it becomes an enterprise that
begins afresh each day, seeking to do God's will, recognizing that

---

[9] Paul L. Lehmann, *Ethics in a Christian Context* (Louisville, KY: Westminster John
Knox, 2006), 45. It is worth noting that Wannenwetsch misreads Lehmann at just
this point. Lehmann does not begin with the church, as Wannenwetsch suspects, but
rather with God. God is the One who establishes the church as the place whereby
men and women become aligned with what he is doing to humanize the world. See
Bernd Wannenwetsch, *Political Worship: Ethics for Christian Citizens*, trans. Margaret
Kohl (Oxford: Oxford University Press, 2004), 55.

[10] Kathryn Tanner, *Christ the Key* (Cambridge: Cambridge University Press, 2010),
51.

the doing of God's will is a matter of being rendered transparent to what God is already doing 'to keep human life *human* in the world'.[11] Ethics is a matter of being transformed, then, such that men and women, the community of faith, learn to will what God wills and so become truly human. Ethics is all about describing a way of being that attests the new thing God is doing – 'the new order' brought into being by Christ's ministry and cross as it is contemporized by his resurrection.[12] To the extent that it does so, there will always be an apocalyptic moment at its heart. Human activity is always a *witness* – that is its status – to the presence of the acting subject, and never as such immediately transparent to Christ. It does not 'make' Christ relevant but rather is continuously summoned to be relevant to him. His presence is perspicuous and luminous, and it is his clarity that overflows onto us whose humanity is in him and is being shaped by him so that it may be true to him.

THE DISPLACEMENT OF CHRISTOLOGY

Throughout the essay I demonstrate that a description of the ethical environment requires a dogmatic, which is to say, a seriously enduring *theological* foundation. This book is an intervention invoked by a problem: the lack of Christology – specifically, reference to the presence and ongoing ministry of Jesus Christ – in contemporary works in Christian and/or theological ethics. Ethics is at times understood to be where individuals or the church begin and, concomitantly, where Jesus leaves off. Four contemporary examples can be cited. Although representing different starting points and traditions of theological thought, in each one there is – to varying degrees – a subtle displacement of Christological doctrine, namely that of William Schweiker, Bernd Wannenwetsch, Samuel Wells and David Cunningham. To be sure, this is not the place to offer a detailed critique of each; however, it is important to refer to some of the animating impulses of some influential contemporary thinkers in the area of Christian ethics, in order to ascertain a sense of the lacunae which this essay addresses.

In the case of William Schweiker, one who is clearly working within the heritage of Paul Tillich, it is not so much a heavy deployment of the doctrine of the church which is the issue but rather a doctrine

---

[11] Lehmann, *Ethics*, 85, original emphasis.
[12] Lehmann, *Ethics*, 123.

of God in which there is minimal Christological content. In his important study, *Responsibility and Christian Ethics*, Schweiker accounts for God in terms of a 'symbol' of Christian faith, 'the self-interpretation of ultimate reality'.[13] For Schweiker:

> God is the symbol in Christian faith for the unconditional course and possibility of moral responsibility. God makes responsibility possible by creating and sustaining the moral space of life. And this means that the imperative of responsibility must be reformulated theocentrically in terms of an integrated ethics of responsibility... In all actions and relations we ought to respect and enhance the integrity of life *before God*.[14]

Although Schweiker is incorporating language from Bonhoeffer's *Ethics*, namely that of 'responsibility' and life lived 'before God', he does not do what Bonhoeffer does, which is to inflect these terms Christologically.[15] To be sure, Schweiker's approach is theocentric in an ongoing sense but not all that Christocentric. Hence my concern with Schweiker is that he defines God in relative abstraction from the life, death, resurrection and ascension of Jesus Christ, apart from the economy of salvation. Accordingly, his account of what we are to do – namely, serve the good of existence – is somewhat thin, then, because it is underwritten by a doctrine of God that lacks particularity and rigorous appeal to Christology.

> Christian faith articulates and interprets the basic experience of responsibility. That experience is the sense that contingent existence is good in its finitude and ought to be respected and enhanced... Christian faith articulates this experience [the basic experience of responsibility before God] in terms of the being of God.[16]

To be sure, Christian faith has much to say about the nature of human responsibility before God and before one another, albeit

---

[13] William Schweiker, *Responsibility and Christian Ethics* (Cambridge: Cambridge University Press, 1995), 208, 210.

[14] Schweiker, *Responsibility*, 208, original emphasis. See also David E. Klemm and William Schweiker, *Religion and the Human Future: An Essay on Theological Humanism* (Malden, MA: Blackwell, 2008).

[15] See *DBW*, vol. 6, *Ethics*, ed. Clifford J. Green (Minneapolis: Fortress Press, 2005), for example the manuscript 'History and Good [1]'. For Bonhoeffer, responsible action lies in God's hands as only God can do the good. God does not render us inert in relationship to the seeking and doing of good. Our actions are good inasmuch as they are in accordance with the reality of Jesus Christ '[who] is the responsible human being par excellence'. Moreover, Bonhoeffer is insistent that life before God is always life before God *in* Jesus Christ, who wills to take form in human historical existence via a life of 'concrete responsible action'. See *Ethics*, 232, 233.

[16] Schweiker, *Responsibility and Christian Ethics*, 226.

to the extent that it takes its cues from the pioneer and perfecter of Christian faith, Jesus Christ. Responsibility thus understood is a matter of acting in accord with reality in an ongoing sense: Jesus Christ, and of becoming participant in his very expansiveness as he seeks to be present to all and in all, transformingly so. Contingent existence ought to be 'enhanced' – although the language of enhancement seems to fall short of primary New Testament language like that of existence being subject to the 'new creation'.[17] Christian faith does not so much articulate an experience of the goodness of contingent existence in terms of God's being, rather than describe and witness to a God whose being is triune, and who exercises his freedom in the second person by becoming human in order to remake humanity – contingent existence – for himself. Accordingly, God is so much more than 'a source and goal of life itself', a 'symbol', and one who creates 'the possibility of moral responsibility'.[18] God, rather, in Jesus Christ through the power of the Spirit, mortifies and vivifies humanity, thereby enacting the new creation – of which Jesus' resurrection is the firstfruits – as the basis of and genuine possibility for moral responsibility that is in accord with the grain of the universe.

Incorporating and at times advancing many of Stanley Hauerwas's best insights, there is the work of Samuel Wells, who in his otherwise helpful book *God's Companions: Reimagining Christian Ethics,* argues that the centre of an account of Christian ethics is to be the 'Church'.[19] While Wells is far more specific about God's identity – unlike Schweiker, he talks in unabashedly trinitarian terms – my concern with Wells is that such a focus on the church bespeaks a kind of 'misplaced concreteness'.[20] Over and against Wells, the practices of the church, I argue, are not to be ethics' centre. Rather, ethics' centre is to be the presence and ongoing ministry of Christ which includes and engenders, of course, practices peculiar to it. In this economy, we encounter a God who in Christ is prophetically present to his people, inviting them to become participants in his reality constituting work via particular creaturely acts: for example, that of

[17] See, for example, 2 Cor. 5.17.

[18] Schweiker, *Responsibility and Christian Ethics,* 226, 208.

[19] Samuel Wells, *God's Companions: Reimagining Christian Ethics* (Malden, MA: Blackwell, 2006), 10. See also Samuel Wells and Ben Quash, *Introducing Christian Ethics* (Malden, MA: Wiley-Blackwell, 2010).

[20] Nicholas M. Healy, 'Misplaced Concreteness? Practices and the New Ecclesiology', *International Journal of Systematic Theology* 5 (Fall 2003): 287–308.

hearing, obedience and service. Although helpful at many points, I
think that Wells's approach would be even more edifying if it were
more thoroughly leavened by the formative power of the reality of
the world constituted by the God of the Gospel. It is this formative
context that is Jesus' person – definitive as it is of reality – which is
lacking, as Wells too quickly attends to what the church is and does,
shortchanging God's activity which in Christ establishes the context
for what the church is and does, and thus what it is that the human
is to be and do.

In the case of an extremely lucid and very recent contribution to
the discipline of Christian ethics, written in a manner which takes
up the language of virtues and of communities as concerns their
import for ethics, David Cunningham's contribution stands at the
fore. As concerns virtues, Cunningham writes, 'Christians understand
the virtues to be those dispositions *God has by nature*, and in which
human beings *can participate by grace*'.[21] Accordingly, Christian ethics
is not a system of morality: it 'resists being reduced to a set of rules
for good behaviour'.[22] Indeed, ethics cannot be reduced to a set of
rules because the call to virtue is a call to embrace and participate in
the grace of God which empowers us to be virtuous people and thus
to have a share in itself. In the case of Cunningham's account, it is
the Christian community which is *formative*, the very place wherein
men and women learn to embrace and participate in what is God's
by nature and can be theirs by grace.

It is important, I think, to note that Cunningham's account,
much like Wells's', has a less than robust Christology as its basis.
This is evident when one attends to his description of the context or
environment in which we act. It is the case, for Cunningham, that
Christ is absent, and that it is our task to make him present. Despite
his very clear insistence that the life of virtue in community is capacitated and sustained by grace, sacramentally mediated, a Pelagian
impulse is nonetheless present in that the human (community)
becomes responsible for realizing the subject of ethics – Jesus Christ.
Says Cunningham:

> But because the teachings of Jesus were offered in a particular historical,
> geographical, and cultural context, *extending* [emphasis mine] them through
> time and space can be a difficult task. The Spirit's work is to guide Christians in

[21] David S. Cunningham, *Christian Ethics: The End of the Law* (London: Routledge,
2008), 167, original emphasis.
[22] Cunningham, *Ethics*, 266.

this task, helping them to make Christ present in other historical and cultural contexts. Consequently, the claim that 'Christ is the end of the law' can be extended into these new contexts, adapting the insights of Jesus to every new historical and geographical circumstance.[23]

While I concur that it is the Spirit who indeed leads and guides men and women in the way of Christ, the Spirit does not in my view lead and guide in the name of a Jesus who is not present. Jesus Christ is present through the Spirit. In Thomas F. Torrance's words, Christ is 'present, really present [through the Spirit], but [present] in a different way'.[24] That different way is simply that Jesus is no longer physically present; rather, he is present through Word and Spirit in the mode of promise. What appears, then, to be terribly disconnected, namely the exigencies of creaturely life in relation to the ascended Christ, are, if Torrance is correct, through the Spirit 'infinitely closely related'.[25] If such is the case, then, there is not a need to burden our action – even if it be understood to be Spirit-empowered action – with that of extending Christ into new contexts. There is only one context: that is Christ whose communicative presence and ongoing ministry is the order of being that is, by him and his Spirit, being brought into being. And so, we see again the basic need for an intervention for which this book is written, that is, the call to understand ethics in a manner appropriate to Jesus' person. This book is a call to consider Christ as present and so ministering, and to consider human life and indeed world history 'in light of the heavenly session and ministry of the heavenly mediator'.[26]

The last case in point, whose orienting impulses and foundation are also ecclesiological, is that of Bernd Wannenwetsch in his dense book *Political Worship: Ethics for Christian Citizens*. To be sure, worship has formative power for Christian ethics, as his section title for Part III of the book indicates. But his book makes worship undertake theological work for which it cannot be responsible unless heavily leavened by a sense of the ongoing presence and activity of Jesus Christ. Worship is a matter of our being drawn by the Spirit into the Son's communion with the Father. However, to declare worship as the act, as does Wannenwetsch, whereby the Christian community

---

[23] Cunningham, *Ethics*, 180. Over and against such a view, Torrance writes, '*The resurrection remains continuous live happening that does not decay into the past.*' *Atonement*, 245, original emphasis.

[24] Torrance, *Atonement*, 305.

[25] Torrance, *Atonement*, 294.

[26] Torrance, *Atonement*, 297.

is constituted a *polis* whose form of existence is dependent upon reconciliation, and whose ethics spring from worship itself, is to champion worship as something of the foundation for ethics. Thus Wannenwetsch: worship is '*the* context *per se* for Christian ethics', for the church is determined by her worship.[27] I would want to say, instead, that the church's context is fundamentally determined by Jesus Christ, the worship of whom is one of the chief acts of obedience undertaken by the Christian community whereby it becomes and more nearly corresponds to what it is and is becoming: the body of Christ. Again, foundation language, when it is applied to the church or the church's activity, displaces somewhat, in Wannenwetsch's case, the active agent and acting subject in an account of the church and of ethics.

Having said that, there are moments in Wannenwetsch's text that indicate recognition of the primacy of the presence of God in Christ through Word and Spirit and its import for ethics. For example, 'Christian ethics *always* has to take its start, over and over again, from the event where human beings are grasped by the self-communication of God'.[28] I concur. What would strengthen Wannenwetsch's already very impressive offering would be a more consistent deference to the Christological character of this self-communication as always being ever present and generative of worship and of acts of obedience. Without that, worship can appear to function as a principle; indeed, it can become somewhat static unless it, too, is robustly situated in the presence and ministry of a person profoundly expansive, so very expansive, in fact, that his person is generative of the praise of creatures. Jesus' presence and ministry, and only then the worship of the church, is the 'central political event' of the church till his Kingdom come in all of its eschatological fullness.[29]

The 'Is' and the 'Ought'

In some of Protestant modernity, it was customary to isolate doctrine from ethics, to speak of the former as if it only belonged to the realm of the theoretical, and thus the latter as if it was the property of more practical considerations. According to this view, doctrines denote staid articulations of a Christ whose person is at best confined to the

---

[27] Wannenwetsch, *Political Worship*, 57, original emphasis.

[28] Wannenwetsch, *Political Worship*, 18, original emphasis.

[29] Wannenwetsch, *Political Worship*, 325.

past, a person who is to be mined for principles which will, hopefully, form the basis for meaningful action in the here and now. This is to say, church doctrine, in our case, Christian teaching on the presence and ongoing ministry of Jesus Christ, is far removed from the vicissitudes of everyday life in late capitalist modernity and is therefore of questionable relevance. That men and women so often think in such a way is indicative of just how infrequently teaching about the presence of Jesus Christ, and what the ascended Christ is doing by the power of the Spirit to establish forms of human life appropriate to his person, is thought of as having ethical import. Jesus may be the pioneer of faith in the sense of faith's example, but certainly not faith's perfecter, the One present to faith by Word and Spirit.

If Christ is indeed the pioneer and perfecter of ethics, it would be apt to attend to his life – as narratively attested – in order to account for the way in which he can be said to be our contemporary. And so, in an essay such as this, it would be presumptuous to account for the presence of Christ's power, truth and love in advance and thus apart from serious theological exegesis. Thus I offer a reading of three moments in the Fourth Gospel. Specifically, I describe the world encountered there as a living world. This is because the acting agent of the narrative of John's Gospel, the historical and crucified Jesus, is, according to the way in which he enacts his identity, therefore present and contemporary.[30]

This Jesus – the Jesus of history – is present because his history never dies: he rose again and ascended. His past is present and also future. Such a notion upsets the dichotomy which reigns in classical historical criticism, with its easy bifurcation of the so-called 'Jesus of history' and the 'Christ of faith'. But let us suppose for a moment that the two are one and the same. To use a more biblical mode of thought, let it be wagered that Jesus Christ fulfills the old covenant and ministers the new covenant. To be sure, Christ's fulfills the old in the most ignominious way imaginable; but the manner of his fulfillment of the old through a cross is the ground of his returning in glory and the basis for his contemporaneity. E. C. Hoskyns calls this 'the contrast' of the Synoptic tradition. 'The contrast is not between the Jesus of history and the Christ of faith, but between the Christ humiliated, and the Christ returning in glory.'[31] I mention

---

[30] See Torrance, *Atonement*, 293.

[31] E. C. Hoskyns, 'The Christ of the Synoptic Gospels', in *Essays Catholic and Critical*, ed. Edward Gordon Selwyn (London: SPCK, 1926), 177.

this because in a book which offers a reading of three key moments in John's Gospel, I work with the assumption that the Jesus narrated there is not any less historical or any less real than the Jesus of the Synoptics. Accordingly, the humble man narratively depicted therein reigns and is present in glory.

John's Gospel does not represent the triumph of foreign – read 'Hellenic' – influences. Rather, the Johannine writings are 'a spontaneous Christian development. The commentator will find that the New Testament is one book, not merely because certain documents have been collected together by ecclesiastical authority or by common Christian usage, but because it presumes an underlying unity of faith and experience'.[32] That underlying unity of faith and experience is the 'permanent and final presence of God in the flesh'.[33] It is God's presence in the flesh which is the basis for canonical unity. What this implies, then, is that it is possible to read the Fourth Gospel in a way that honors the past and the present and indeed the future: that what the person of Jesus did then, in first-century Palestine, Jesus does now and will do.[34]

Teaching on the person of Christ offers the Christian community – the church – a concrete norm. This is to say, an account of the presence and ongoing ministry of Jesus Christ is an account that describes *who* it is who claims men and women in his Gospel, not only revealing himself to them but turning them to himself. Again, he is the author *and* perfecter of faith. He is the 'is' and, in the Spirit, the 'ought'; Christ's presence has ethical import. If such is the case, then, Christology has directive power. If we confess and believe God's power, truth and love are in Jesus Christ demonstrated in a particular human way, then we will not remain unchanged; for we will also have described how God's truth, love and power in Jesus Christ brings itself to bear on human existence, rendering humanity, in faith, permeable to such truth, love and power. One of the most important Christian – which is to say, theological – ethicists of the latter part of the twentieth century, the late Reformed thinker Paul L. Lehmann, in his brilliant but difficult book *Ethics in a Christian Context*, puts it this way: doctrine supplies 'materials for a theological

[32] Hoskyns, 'Synoptic Gospels', in *Essays*, 178.

[33] Torrance, *Atonement*, 302.

[34] There is an 'eschatological reserve' to be sure, the notion that he is not yet fully manifest in glory. Were he present to his disciples, or for that matter to us, in such a way, 'They [and we] would have been damned on the spot'. See Torrance, *Atonement*, 434.

analysis of ethics'.[35] In this essay, I do not intend to analyze ethics in terms of the question of 'What shall we do?' but rather to go a step further, and so to describe ethical acts as acts that, one hopes, are acts participant in the presence of the hypostatic union of God and humanity in Jesus Christ.

Lehmann noted well over a generation ago that 'contemporary discussions of Christian ethics have been notably careless at this point [at the point of Christology and of neglecting doctrine in general]'.[36] My lament – and it is really but footnotes to Lehmann's – is that so often works in Christian ethics abandon theology proper, becoming principally a matter of formulating response(s) to what God has done, rather than of attending to ethics from the side of Christ who instills through Word and Spirit the power, truth and love of himself into us, and is as such the obedient answer to that power, truth and love, an answer which takes us up, rendering us correspondent to it. Ethics is indeed not our own undertaking. What I am arguing, then, is that the kind of God the Gospel gives us is the starting and end point for ethics, for it is this God who in Christ by the Spirit not only turns to us but turns us to himself, freeing us to live in fellowship with himself and with one another, and in so doing has set and sets us upon a path by which we may do precisely that. Ethics are our fumbling response to Jesus' contemporary ministry, a ministry that takes place in power, truth and love, a ministry which through his Spirit is realized in us.

Although this essay is not concerned with extensive description of the details of moral life, it is mindful that a moral ontology does not exclude concentration on the details of moral life. It is simply to acknowledge that all of life is subject to the presence and doings of a person who humanizes. That I do not go into explicit description of moral policy particulars regarding this humanizing presence is not a deficiency, but rather the attempt to situate the 'What shall we do?' kinds of questions in the light of a larger cosmological action making all things new.

The divine economy, the totality of God's doings, their culmination in the life, passion, death, resurrection, ascension and heavenly session of Christ function as the principle of intelligibility for ethics. Together these moments point to 'the meaning and direction of

---

[35] Lehmann, *Ethics*, 104.

[36] The point he has in mind is ethics' 'christological foundation'. See Lehmann, *Ethics*, 104.

the divine behaviour, and thus also of human behaviour'.[37] In other words, to talk or to describe the things of God in Christ as effective in the Spirit is not to exclude ourselves, but rather to talk about how we have been caught up into God's gracious dealings with humankind in Christ by the Spirit. Indeed, humanity is never to be conceived apart from the eternal Son who in the fullness of time has assumed flesh and is at work drawing all to himself.

Once we have a sense of the economy of grace in which we are situated and of the identity of the one who situates us in it, we can then be 'on the way toward the new humanity to be consummated in the "second Adam" and the "second Advent" '.[38] Stated somewhat differently, attention to the identity of the one disclosed in the economy of grace means attention, too, to how humanity is itself brought into a new state of affairs. Such a humanity is a humanity which acknowledges that a fundamentally new reality has been brought into being, apart from any doing of its own, and that that state of affairs is indicative of reality itself. The shape of the new humanity is thus given concrete direction in identity descriptions of the person of Jesus Christ, in that these descriptions of the power, truth and love he is license acts that serve to bring us into conformity to the new state of affairs into which we have been placed and are through the Spirit being placed. Indeed, Christ Jesus is present in such a way that his own annihilation of sin and death might attain its true end in us. 'It is no longer I who live, but it is Christ who lives in me' (Gal. 2.20).

CHRISTOLOGY AND CONTEXT

Another important insight of Lehmann's is that what God is doing in the world offers 'a radical transvaluation of the context, meaning, and direction of life in this world, and accordingly of human behaviour'.[39] It is possible to map the context – the environment of ethical decision – only in light of God. Christ's presence provides, to take up Lehmann's language, a certain kind of direction for human life, rooted in the reconciliation that is the new reality for human life.[40] Stated differently, the activity of God is germane to the reality

[37] Lehmann, *Ethics*, 105.
[38] Lehmann, *Ethics*, 107.
[39] Lehmann, *Ethics*, 111.
[40] See also Karl Barth, *Church Dogmatics*, ed. T. F. Torrance and G. W. Bromiley

of human life. It is activity that includes us by judging us and our wayward ways and thereby sets us upon a new path and a new context, and impels us in a new direction. God points human life in the world in this way and not that way, that is, in a way of being that is generative of a new life in conformity to God's will which is life. But we will only be cognizant of that new way inasmuch as we attend to its ground and reality, that is, God's fellowship creating activity in Jesus Christ. This activity truly teaches us about the shape of God's power, truth and love by being our very response to it: Jesus Christ is the human response to God in which we participate by faith. It is Jesus' contemporary ministry, the ministry of him who is really One with us in our humanity, that grounds ethics and is the place from which ethics proceeds and by which it is sustained.

Jesus Christ establishes reality, what is really real, and directs and renders men and women in the way of that which is really real. Indeed, the various actualities or contexts in which we find ourselves are in desperate need of transvaluation by God, by a new kind of 'principle of intelligibility'. Indeed, what we think of as power, truth and love is very often thought of in immanentist terms, that is, as if the world were a closed place, impervious to the judging and pardoning action of God in Christ. Thus truth, love and power, defined on our terms become functions of power plays we engage in to survive a hyper-competitive late modern world. Therefore, dogmatic treatment of Christ's presence as a new 'principle of intelligibility' describes the context, meaning and direction of human life as if life were not the property of the human or subservient to a global capitalist economic system, but rather the gift of a God who freely and effectively turns to us in the covenant of grace and thereby turns us to him through that same history, directing us in the way of life.

When Lehmann says that doctrine offers 'a radical transvaluation of the context', he is, moreover, indicating that the context in which we find ourselves is not transparent unto itself, nor does it provide directives. The context or field in which we find ourselves requires theology – specifically, Christology – for its intelligibility. What the Christian community is to do is, in any given state of affairs, call upon the name of the Lord, rather than assume that its context will – without a Word from outside – provide it with the resources and directions for appropriate action. Stated differently, there is only one

(hereafter cited as *CD*), vol. IV/2, *The Doctrine of Reconciliation* (Edinburgh: T&T Clark, 1958), §64.4, 'The Direction of the Son'.

Word we must hear in all 'contexts' in life and in death, and that Word is Jesus Christ. This book is an attempt to hear that Word in all of his eternality, contemporaneity and promeity. The contours of the community's context remain opaque apart from such hearing. Hearing teaches not only dependence, but also teaches us to wait upon the Lord whose Word illuminates the context and clarifies it, giving to the individual and community within a given context a perspicacity with respect to the context it never possessed before. The context is thus able to be rightly understood as not only the simple set of contingencies in which we find ourselves, imprisoned as we are by the fallenness of our first parents to which we freely accede, but also as illumined by what is the life-giving work of God in Christ and determined by God's history and will with us.[41] That work and the character of the God who does that work provides us with the spectacles by which we see the context aright and the sanctified will by which we act in that context aright in a manner transparent to the One by whom we see.

Christology provides the context for human life as men and women come, through the preaching and sacraments of the church, to appreciate the new world in which they live, and the character of this new world which brings itself to bear on their conduct and behavior, as those who are 'bearers of the new humanity which in Christ has become a fact in the world and in which, in consequence of who Christ is and what he is doing in the world, we participate'.[42] Without this focus, that is the 'fact' of the new humanity in Christ in which we participate by the obedience of faith, it becomes all too easy to suggest that Christ's presence is not actually ongoingly operative and effective. For example, Graham Ward writes,

> The presence of Christ with us now is discerned in the Eucharist within every act of faith, among the congregation of the faithful, analogically in every identi-fication of justice, peace, love, joy, and community. The operations of Christ's presence is found in every identified manifestation and every recognition of the gifts of the Spirit... It is an index of the mysterious – that is, the sacramental excess that invests the everyday reality of things.[43]

What I would like to have heard, and what I offer in this essay, is a stronger sense of the reality and ongoing presence and ministry of

[41] See John Webster, *Word and Church: Essays in Dogmatics I* (Edinburgh: T&T Clark, 2001), 4–5.

[42] Lehmann, *Ethics*, 119.

[43] Graham Ward, *The Politics of Discipleship: Becoming Postmaterial Citizens* (Grand Rapids, MI: Baker Academic, 2009), 170.

Jesus Christ. Discernment language, while there is a place for such, suggests Christ's presence to be that which may require actualization. It is my view that Christ's presence is discerned first and foremost via his Word, the apostolic testimony, the promises of which are sealed in the Eucharist as the Spirit works to create a people transparent to them. This essay is, 'in consequence of what God in Christ is doing', an attempt to sketch the power, truth and love of Christ in all of its objective *and* subjective splendor: 'God with us [the objective] means we with God [the subjective].'[44] That we undertake to do the hard work of actual description of the concrete character of the presence of Christ's power, truth and love as revealed in the economy of grace will, one can only hope, ensure the priority always remains his reality in all of its expansiveness, his reality understood as generative of ethics and thus of moral agency.

OUTLINE OF THE MAIN CHAPTERS

In each of the three main chapters of the text, I do four things. First, when it comes to the presence of Christ's power (Chapter 2), truth (Chapter 3), and love (Chapter 4), I attend to Scripture, specifically John's Gospel. In Chapter 2, I offer a reading of Jesus' healing of a sick man (John 5.1-18), in Chapter 3 a reading of the trial scenes (John 18.1–19.16), and in Chapter 4 a reading of the resurrection appearance to the seven disciples (John 21).[45] In reading the narrative, I understand, following Hans Frei, the narrative and the meaning, as was the case in precritical exegesis, to bear significantly on each other.[46] The meaning of John's Gospel is not something different from the narrative sequence. Accordingly, my concern is not to go behind the text but rather to attend to the texts at hand as texts that interrogate us, their readers, as a 'counter-Word'.[47] This is to say, I read John's Gospel as a text that originates in a particular context and set of circumstances, but which transcends its occasionality by virtue of it being annexed to the acting Agent of the narrative's self-attestation. These texts (a healing episode, the trial scenes, and the resurrection appearances) speak then, not because they hold some

[44] Torrance, *Atonement*, 168.

[45] I use the NRSV translation.

[46] See Hans W. Frei, *The Eclipse of Biblical Narrative* (New Haven, CT: Yale University Press, 1974), 16.

[47] See further Bonhoeffer, *Christ the Center*, 27, 28.

intrinsic power of their own, but rather because the One whom they narrate is present and has elected them as the form of his own speech. He lives as the one who is depicted there.

Thus I take for granted the unity of the life and teaching of Jesus in the Synoptic Gospels with that of John. Although the emphases of the Synoptics are different than those of John and those of John different than the Synoptics, I would not want to suggest that the former are more historical and the latter more theological. The relation between them is one of deep inner unity, for it is the same subject who is being attested.[48] Four portraits, not one, are necessary to capture this subject in all his fullness. The reason why the canonical Gospels live and speak is that Jesus lives; but the way in which he can be said to live and to be present as One who lives eternally knows no precise parallel.[49] And so, these texts live as texts that read us because the One of whom they speak is risen and ascended, and so is present among us as the resurrected Lord who acts now in agreement with how he acted then. The aim in the first section of each of the main chapters, then, is to offer a reading of a given moment in John's Gospel in such a way that greater Christological specificity be lent to George Lindbeck's maxim: 'It is the text, so to speak, which absorbs the world, rather than the world the text.'[50] The texts do absorb our world, indeed; but they absorb it precisely because these texts belong to Another, as the instrument by which he absorbs us and renders us his contemporaries and aligns us to what he is doing.

I also think it important in an essay on Christ's presence and ministry and on ethics as the human being's answering righteousness to Christ's presence that Scripture be read. A text on Christology

[48] This is my 'response' to the problem as posed by E. C. Hoskyns: 'What is the relation between the life and teaching of Jesus of Nazareth and the Christ of St. Paul, of St. John, and of Catholic piety?' The answer, in short, is that we need not go behind the text of the Synoptics in order to discover Jesus' real history. Rather, the Synoptics present a view of history in relation to which John is 'a spontaneous Christian development'. Hoskyns, 'Synoptic Gospels', in *Essays*, 153, 178.

[49] In Hans Frei's words, 'Neither person nor circumstances can be abstracted from each other. They are not symbolic but unsubstitutably what they are and gain all their significance from being this specific set and no other, and from the interconnection between this unsubstitutable person with these circumstances. He alone is at their centre and lends them their character.' Hans W. Frei, *The Identity of Jesus Christ: With Theological Reflections on the Accounts of Jesus' Death and Resurrection* (Eugene, OR: Wipf and Stock, 1997), 36.

[50] George A. Lindbeck, *The Nature of Doctrine: Religion and Theology in a Postliberal Age* (Philadelphia: Westminster Press, 1984), 118.

and ethics cannot afford to be exegetically thin, precisely because Christology is a description of the person who acts as narratively depicted, and ethics an account of what the One who acts as Scripturally attested would have of us. This is not an essay that champions an abstract environment for ethics: Scripture occupies a normative role in the construal of ethical reality. It seeks to account for ethics in relationship to Holy Scripture, seeking to bridge what is perceived to be the unbridgeable gap between the 'then and there' and the 'here and now' with Scripture, Scripture read as an account of what Jesus is now doing. His contemporary ministry, in other words, is his past ministry in the first century as contemporized by his resurrection and ascension. Hence time needs to be taken to attend to his actual ministry, and to ask in what way his person and ministry lives. And so, the first section in Chapters 2, 3 and 4, respectively, is one that reads given moments of Jesus' history as moments that travel 'within and through our historical existence'.[51]

The second section of each of the three main chapters is devoted to dogmatic description of Christ's enacted identity with a view to an articulation of his eternality *and* contemporaneity, the former being the ground of the latter. Presence is a function of identity, and so this second section accounts for the identity of Christ's power, truth and love in a way that attends to its eternality and only then its contemporaneity.[52] The second section of Chapters 2, 3 and 4 thus asks a series of simple questions: *Who* is this one who acted and acts? And to what extent is his action in fulfilling Israel's history a reiteration of his eternal identity? Also, to what extent is his action in the economy, precisely as rooted in his eternality, contemporary? Is his contemporaneity a function of his person as eternal? I think this discussion important because when Christology is considered in ethics – which is too rare, it seems – its economic aspects are often privileged. The considerable moral force of the immanent life of the Son is rarely honored. The One who is *pro nobis* 'displays the sovereign *self*-disposal of God for the sake of his creatures'.[53] The immanent aspects of Christology do matter, then, precisely because they point to the *freedom* of the One who is indeed *pro me*. Bonhoeffer's edifying

---

[51] Torrance, *Atonement*, 170.

[52] See Frei, *Identity*, 77.

[53] See Philip G. Ziegler, 'Promeity in the Christologies of Bonhoeffer and Kierkegaard' (paper presented at the Annual Meeting of the American Academy of Religion, Atlanta, GA, 31 October 2010), original emphasis.

insistence on Christ's promeity can only be strengthened by an
account of Christ's eternality as the One who is free to be this way
precisely because he *is* this way; he is this person.

Furthermore, the taking up of immanent aspects of Christology
is important for herein is the place where an account of reality
appropriate to Jesus' presence and ministry – as the eternal One –
arises. If Bonhoeffer is indeed correct in insisting that God's reality is
revealed in Jesus Christ, then Christ's person, Christ's identity, is the
foundation of all reality.[54] But not only is it the foundation, it wills to
become real in all that there is. So the eternal Christ is the author of
reality, the agent of creation and salvation, and as the eternal Christ
is the One who perfects reality, achieves reality in us.[55] Just *who* is it
who not only establishes reality but also wills that his enacted identity
– which is not the obviation of the creature but instead the creature's
genuine exaltation – become real, be perfected in all that there is?
This second section, in other words, is nothing but an answer to
that question by describing what *is* in an ontic sense on the basis of
the (eternal) identity enacted in John 5.1-18; John 18.1–19.10; and
John 21.

If the second section of each main chapter be devoted to the *is*,
then the third takes up the 'ought' via the language of command. If
Jesus is indeed our human response to God,[56] converting humanity
from estrangement to friendship with God by the power of the Spirit,
then what kind of ethical vitality and significance can the presence
of his power, truth and love be said to have? In order to answer
this question, I invoke the language of command, specifically the
command of power, truth and love. Such language once again is not
meant to suggest that ethics – human action in obedience to the
command – is our undertaking. The ought is not first and foremost
about us. Rather, the 'ought', as the command, is ingredient in the
'is', the one who is present in the Spirit in power, truth and love.
Accordingly, this third section is an exploration of the sense that
his presence has ethical vitality concretely via his command. It is to

[54] *DBW*, vol. 6, *Ethics*, 49.

[55] Jaroslav Pelikan, *The Christian Tradition: A History of the Development of Doctrine*, vol.
1, *The Emergence of the Catholic Tradition (100–600)* (Chicago: University of Chicago
Press, 1971), 205.

[56] I have in mind Galatians 2.20 as translated with the objective genitive: the 'faith of
Christ'. For further debate on this point, see Michael F. Bird and Preston M. Sprinkle,
eds. *The Faith of Christ: Exegetical, Biblical, and Theological* (Peabody, MA: Hendrickson,
2010).

say that the One who pioneers power, truth and love by virtue of his presence is the One who in the Spirit perfects it via his command.

In describing Christ's presence also as law or command, this is not to suggest that he relinquishes, even for a moment, his agency in achieving what he is in us via his command. What he commands, we do indeed obey – albeit provisionally – in him. His truth is revealed in our flesh, 'done into our flesh' as Torrance would say, and it is also answered in our flesh.[57] So an account of the command ingredient as the presence of Christ's power, truth and love is to point out how the acting Subject *achieves* his faithfulness, his ministry, among us – 'Christ in you, the hope of glory' – via his command.[58] His presence in power, truth and love has directive significance, and it has this by virtue of the command he is. Stated differently, Christ in the core of his person is also a 'Do this'. Accordingly, what I will give in the penultimate section of each of the three main chapters is an account of the imperative character of his presence via the category of command.

Furthermore, command is crucial to my account, not least because of Bonhoeffer's remarkably trenchant account of the command of God in his *Ethics*, but also because command is a salutary and nonetheless neglected theological category that does remarkable justice to how God's gift of himself, his presence and ministry in Christ, includes a task which gives direction. In more technical terms, you might say that Christ bears the Spirit whom he receives from his Father, that the Gospel includes law, that which turns us to the Law-Giver and enables us to fully live in light of his presence as the very obedience of what he gives. In David Haddorff's words, 'The gospel takes "priority over the law" because it declares firmly what God has done *for* us in Jesus Christ; this is the content of the gospel. In contrast, the law as form of the gospel tells us what we must do *for* God, but only after considering the content of the gospel, of God's reconciliation of the sinner.'[59]

If section one be Bible; two be Gospel, that is, a description of reality inflected in light of the eternal Son become Son of Man; section three reflection upon the moral force of Christ's ministering presence via his commandment, then section four will be

---

[57] Torrance, *Atonement*, 83.

[58] Col. 1.27.

[59] David Haddorff, *Christian Ethics as Witness: Barth's Ethics for a World at Risk* (Eugene, OR: Cascade, 2010), 108, original emphasis.

reflection upon the previous threefold account's moral significance. The language of significance sounds perhaps deliberately vague. But this is where I ask after the pastoral and moral policy particulars of the presence of such power, truth and love. The language of moral or even pastoral particulars is a way of speaking to the new kind of situation that is being perfected in accordance with the previous dogmatic description. While not going into great detail surrounding the specifics of moral policy, this section is an attempt to demonstrate once again that what is being championed is not an ontology that simply falls on us with a thud. In this section, to use Bonhoeffer's language, I reflect 'not "religiously"' on the details of the moral life lived in the presence of such power, truth and love.[60]

To think 'not "religiously"' is to account for the significance of the operative presence – the self-involvement – of Christ with respect to everyday existence, the location of ourselves and our world in his presence and time.[61] It is an attempt to think about presence in a way that takes seriously that God in Christ is not 'everywhere or to everyone present *in the same way*'.[62] Indeed, it is a matter, as is the case in the chapter on power, of talking about the presence of Christ's power in relationship to questions of theodicy, such as those raised by the terrible tsunami of 26 December 2004. Stated differently, the task in this last section is to reflect on the significance of a presence that appears on any number of levels to be absence. Indeed, it is to ask after how Christ's seeming absence involves a renewed appreciation of the advent and promissory character of his presence. In this connection, Ingolf U. Dalferth writes, 'The sense of God's *presence* is not the denial or negation of God's absence but, on the contrary, a sense of *God's* presence is possible only because of it: Only because God is absent (i.e. cannot be identified) in a worldly way, God can be acknowledged in the world to be present *as God*.'[63] Inflected Christologically, the task of this section will be to describe the presence of Jesus Christ – which

---

[60] *DBW*, vol. 8, *Letters and Papers*, 428. 'The world *does* need to be understood in a better way than it does itself! But not "religiously", the way the religious socialists want to do.'

[61] See *DBW*, vol. 8, *Letters and Papers*, 428.

[62] Ingolf U. Dalferth, 'God, Time, and Orientation: "Presence" and "Absence" in Religious and Everyday Discourse', in *The Presence and Absence of God: Claremont Studies in the Philosophy of Religion Conference 2008*, ed. Ingolf U. Dalferth (Tübingen: Mohr Siebeck, 2009), 11, original emphasis.

[63] Dalferth, 'God', in *Presence and Absence*, 17, original emphasis.

very much strikes us as absence and silence – in the world as *God's presence* with a view to what this might imply for pressing moral and therewith pastoral particulars.

In the concluding chapter, Chapter 5, I will reflect on the way in which I have used Holy Scripture, specifically Scripture's construal of ethical reality. This essay is a deliberately Scriptural one. By exegeting portions of the Fourth Gospel to find my way around the material, I make what I hope is an important point: Scripture construes ethical reality by informing our sense of what 'is'. Indeed, Scripture does not so much 'absorb' our world as continually place us – inasmuch as we hear – before the real world. Scripture depicts and construes the real world. It is ethics' center. The language of 'absorbing' in a way deflects attention from what is the real issue: namely the way in which these texts are used by the present Christ in the Spirit to bespeak the 'goings on' to which we are subject and into which we are incorporated.

CONCLUSION: AGAINST EXEMPLARISM

The basic aim in this essay is to draw the life of the Christian community into the orbit of the presence and ongoing ministry of Christ, its natural environment, and thus to explore the consequences of his presence for ethics and offer an account of the moral landscape of ethics that is dependent on its environment. Put again, I describe and hear anew, I trust, the character of the revealed power, truth and love of God present in Christ, so as to enable us to participate in a manner befitting our humanity in the presence of that power, truth and love. To do so is to give a firm dogmatic – that is, a theological – foundation for behavior, of the environment in which the Christian and, in turn, the Christian community, lives and moves. To take up Torrance's thought, it is to view reconciliation – which is Christ's person and work – as 'not only once and for all completed and effected, but as travelling within and through our historical existence, as it were, as continually operative in reconciling intervention within history and all the affairs of humanity'.[64] This is an essay that describes ethics as a function of Christ's presence and ministry 'continually operative in reconciling intervention'. Indeed, the Lord Jesus through his Word and Spirit never ceases shaping the Christian community and beyond it the world. The emphasis always then ought to be upon the acting

---

[64] Torrance, *Atonement*, 170.

subject whose agency is never exhausted but continues to have its way by working what he is, by the power of the Spirit, into us.

Only by so doing can the exemplarist dragon that so often rears its head in ethics be slain. By exemplarism I mean the idea that Jesus himself is an example or an instantiation of something that lies beyond himself. He becomes the paradigm, for instance, for talking about social justice or for what personal piety in the religious life might look like. What matters, according to such understandings, is not so much who he is in all his unsubstitutability, but what he can point us toward, something which can be usually found in other 'savior figures' too. In other words, it is what he espouses, and not so much who he actually is in his person and what he accordingly does, that is of importance. What also renders exemplarism so problematic is that it is insensitive 'to what God *is* [emphasis mine] doing in the world to make and to keep human life human, to achieve the maturity of men, that is, the new humanity'.[65] Exemplarism in Christian ethics trades upon principles and a dead Jesus, a Jesus who lives only inasmuch as his example guides. Exemplarism is imprisoned by immanence, the idea that the resources we need for good conduct, for living humanly, are present within the matrix of our own experience, so that Jesus himself is called upon only inasmuch as he corroborates values and attitudes commensurate with our account of what it means to be 'ethical'.

The approach I am championing aims to demonstrate the difference that it makes to ethics when one takes seriously that the God who acted *then* in Christ is confessed to be present to us *now* in Christ through the Word and by the power of the Spirit. This God is not present in any generic way, but in an utterly effective way as One who is ministering. This God is present to our contexts, and issues directives to our contexts via the moral force of his presence understood as command. Indeed, his action seeks to draw all in, rendering us fit participants in it through the Spirit. And his Word summons men and women to obedience via the commandment he gives, so that their lives and in turn the life of the world can witness in the here and now what is new, that is, the form of the new humanity brought into being by God in Christ through the Spirit, the form of humanity that is in accord with what is coming to be.

By the Word, it is indeed given to us what to do. For the Word incarnate, written and proclaimed – and not the context – is that

[65] Lehmann, *Ethics*, 117.

through which God speaks, transformingly so. Christological dogma has directive significance because it believes that God speaks through his Word – Jesus Christ – and thus to the context in which the Word is heard. One could argue, in somewhat different terms, that this book is something of an exercise in first things, namely description of the presence and ongoing ministry of Christ – the enactment of what he is – as the field in which Christians live, move and have our being in ever increasing – one hopes – permeability to his.

An approach rooted in hearing is above all else eschatological – 'apocalyptic', to use fashionable language – in that it asks just what an account of the actions appropriate to the power, truth and love of God present in Christ might look like, if the account really took seriously the basic truth that God's whole history with us is demonstrative of One who *speaks* today through the Law, the prophets, and most definitively his Son, whose person is as such an imperative, command and summons. God's command, whereby we learn to hear the imperatival character of God's speech, also reminds us of the eschatological orientation of ethics. Hearing that is true hearing – hearing that in pointing us to the One who acted savingly helps us to know and to see him as acting thus – will be the hearing of a command that summons the human to live as if this world is indeed the world subject to the restorative judgment and world-renewing pardon of God in Christ.

In sum, this essay offers an account of Christ's presence with a view to unfolding the character of his ministering presence as power, truth and love, and what that might entail for ethics. The indicative or pioneering and imperative or perfecting character of the identity and presence of Christ is appreciated, inasmuch as we understand the context in which we find ourselves to be permeable to the ongoing redemptive activity of God and to indeed be shaped by it. If human life is re-contextualized by God's fellowship creating and humanizing activity in Christ, then it is possible for there to be actions which point, or better, which conform and summon us to the world as it really exists. That world is a world which has a Lord who breathes the Spirit and who commands us to do as he is. Our joy is to believe that he who has rectified all things before God is our contemporary, calling us through acts of service, hearing and obedience, to become participant in his present ministry and advent rule of power, truth and love.

Chapter 2

ON THE PRESENCE OF CHRIST'S POWER

Jesus Christ *is* present as God's power come among us. His presence as power is in agreement with his identity as the agent of creation and of salvation. By reading afresh John 5.1-18, that is, Jesus' healing of an unnamed sick man, we see his power as the agent of new creation at work, the power he indeed is as the Son of the Father. In reading the narrative, we notice, moreover, that his presence before the man is not without its effect: Jesus restores the man's health, effecting the renewal of his body in a way that points to who he is: the presence of God's new creation come among us. By attending, then, to John's witness, we find more than ample grounds for reflecting on the identity of the one who acts thus, which is to gloss the ways in which this simple healing episode gives insight into the powerful character of his present ministry. Christ is acting now among us no less power-fully than he did then; he is present among us by the Spirit in accord with the grain of the universe. In light of Christ's self-presentation as one who has power over forces that dehumanize, is it appropriate, I argue, to also speak of a command which issues forth from this display of his healing power. Indeed, it is fitting and right to argue that the One who presents himself there – as powerful to overcome the forces of sickness and death – implicates us in his self-presentation in such a way that his self-presentation can be said to have moral force. The command ingredient in the narrative is the command to live trans-parently to the new creation he effects, which wills to be actualized in us as *belief.* In offering an account of the identity of the One who is present and ministering in a manner that includes a 'Do this', the opportunity also arises to reflect on the moral significance of the presence of One who is power and acts powerfully to heal. In particular, what might the moral function, the pastoral significance of such an account be with respect to the question of theodicy? If we do indeed believe that the risen and ascended Jesus is present and thus ministering in the Spirit, how might such a framework recast concerns represented under the overarching schema of theodicy?

John's Witness to Power

The Healing of the Sick Man: John 5.1-18

It is appropriate to begin a chapter on the character of Jesus' presence among us in power with a theological reading of some of the most arresting statements of his self-presentation in the fifth and, to a lesser extent, twentieth chapters of John's Gospel. I say appropriate because it would be much easier to begin with a settled and domesticated account of power that is not subject to the withering but ultimately life-giving critique that Holy Scripture provides. For it is Scripture, the appointed instrument through which God addresses and forms his people, that we – God's people – need to hear ever anew. We need to hear it anew so as to have our minds renewed in accord with the presentation of true power and so what true power would have of us. Indeed, we need to immerse ourselves once again in what Karl Barth once called 'The strange new world within the Bible'.[1] Although I cannot and do not intend to supply an exhaustive account of a reading of John 5, what I do is gloss several verses, making the case that the power manifest in Jesus' life is precisely the power that is at work among us and contemporary to us by virtue of his having been raised from the dead and of his breathing of the Spirit.

Before I begin making some comments on the text of the Fourth Gospel itself, let me very briefly explain what it is that God does with this text. First, in Lesslie Newbigin's words, 'By "the text" [of Scripture] I mean the text as it stands, whatever conclusions I may reach about the way by which and the writers and editors by whom it was brought to its present form.'[2] Following Newbigin, my concern is not to go behind the final canonical form of the text, in order to discover the 'historical' kernel, the so-called historical Jesus. This is a Jesus whom many scholars regard as obscured by the husk that is John's imaginative and speculative Christological fancies. Over and

---

[1] See Barth, 'Strange New World', in *Word of God and the Word of Man*.

[2] Lesslie Newbigin, *The Light Has Come: An Exposition of the Fourth Gospel* (Grand Rapids, MI: Eerdmans, 1982), viii.

against such an understanding, I take the view that the final form of
the text is the instrument through which God speaks by the power
of the Spirit so as to bring men and women into agreement with
the truth that is Jesus Christ. That is what Christ does with this text.
My stance toward Scripture is that Scripture is 'a field of divine self-
communication'.[3] Accordingly, John's Gospel can be said to have an
explicit theological agenda insofar as it is an agenda that God has
annexed such that it serves God's will to be known, loved, served and
praised. It follows, then, that I intend to read the text in accordance
with its own evangelical purpose: 'That you may come to believe that
Jesus is the Messiah, the Son of God, and that through believing you
may have life in his name' (John 20.31).

A strange and new kind of power is at work in Jesus' healing of a
crippled man at the Pool on the Sabbath as recorded in John 5.1-18.
This little story identifies Jesus to be one who heals. Attending to this
healing is important for it is as such 'an actual confrontation of men
and women with the presence of God'.[4] That the Gospels – both the
Synoptics and John – are deeply concerned with healing episodes is
not an accident. Indeed, that 'one-fifth of all the material in the four
Gospels is concerned with the healing of physical disease' is key to
helping us identify just *who* it is who is present and at work.[5] Jesus is a
healer, and his healing is, in this instance, of the man 'who had been
ill for thirty-eight years' (John 5.5). That Jesus is a healer indicates to
us that he does not will that life go on as normal for this man whom
he encounters. The healing of the man is a sign, a sign of 'the End',
namely the eschatological enfleshment 'of God's glory and presence
to Israel'.[6] The End denotes, in particular, the culmination of God's
salutary purposes for his creatures. That Jesus heals an ill man is
a very concrete sign that bespeaks God's present and anticipates
God's advent rule wherein the power of evil which manifests itself in
sickness is vanquished, and that all things be rendered transparent
to God's Sabbath rest. Evil as manifested in this man's illness has
indeed met its end: Jesus Christ. Jesus Christ abolishes what distorts,
disfigures and corrupts the creatures whom he and his Father love.
'Stand up, take your mat and walk' (John 5.8).

---

[3] John Webster, *Holy Scripture: A Dogmatic Sketch* (Cambridge: Cambridge University Press, 2003), 104.

[4] Newbigin, *Exposition*, 62.

[5] Newbigin, *Exposition*, 63.

[6] E. C. Hoskyns, *The Fourth Gospel* (London: Faber and Faber, 1940), 1:291; and David Stubbs, 'Returning to the Wilderness' (unpublished manuscript, July 2010).

What is most instructive in the narrative is the effect that Jesus' words have: his words are 'immediately effective'.[7] They are words through which God's presence, God's ongoing rule, breaks forth once again into his chosen people's and indeed his world's history. Through Jesus the one true God '*would accomplish his divine purpose*' and indeed does.[8] The presence of Jesus is powerful: powerful inasmuch as the words he utters accomplish what they purport to do: heal. This gives us a most basic insight into the nature of the power at work and present in Jesus' life, power that is most resplendent in his glorious resurrection from the dead. The power at work in Jesus is the power of the One whom he calls his Father. ' "My Father is still working, and I also am working" ' (John 5.17). Jesus' power to heal *is* the healing power of his Father. It is power that never ceases to be at work, never ceases to 'attack...the whole power of evil which manifests itself both in sickness and in sin'.[9]

In the healing of the man whose name we will never know, we get a glimpse of the logic of Jesus' healing ministry. It is a ministry of giving life and of judging. In John 5.1-18, Jesus gives life to an ill man. His giving of life indicates God's judgment of all that is not commensurate with God's rule of life. Jesus' healing ministry attests, moreover, his identity as One in whom God's life-giving rule *is* present and effective. And so, he judges the man's sickness and thereby takes it away. Indeed, if we look toward the end of the Gospel, we will learn that Jesus goes so far as to allow himself to be nailed to the cross to 'finish' it – all that is not in accord with the new creation and the Sabbath rest – once and for all.[10]

There is more: his healing of the ill man is the occasion for instruction in Jesus' relation to his Father whose work of judging and of giving life *is* Jesus' work. 'In the work of Jesus the Jews are confronted by the work of God.'[11] The God of Israel's work is contemporary to them in the presence and ministry of the man Jesus. Thus a very particular kind of relationship exists between Jesus' work and that of the Father's. Jesus says, 'The Son can do nothing on his own, but only what he sees the Father doing; for whatever the Father does, the Son does likewise' (John 5.19). Father and Son are united in a

[7] Hoskyns, *Fourth Gospel*, 1:294.
[8] Marcus J. Borg and N. T. Wright, *The Meaning of Jesus: Two Visions* (New York: HarperCollins, 1999), 50, original emphasis.
[9] Newbigin, *Exposition*, 64.
[10] See John 19.30.
[11] Hoskyns, *Fourth Gospel*, 1:296.

profound filial relationship of love and obedience. The Son obeys the Father and in so doing attests his love for the Father. That the Son is self-effacing is testimony to the Father's unity with the Son: a Father who does not will to do his will apart from his dearly beloved with whom he is one. That they do the same thing indicates, to gesture toward creedal developments, their ontic unity.

The mission of the Son of God in the Fourth Gospel is that of doing 'likewise': the Son does what the Father is doing. The former 'reproduces the thought and action' of the latter.[12] Jesus' identity is as that of One who does what his Father *is* doing. And what is his Father doing and thus he himself doing, even now? Judging sickness, announcing it as incommensurate with his Father's eschatological rule of life. This is the power of God according to the narrative. Jesus manifests in the healing of the man just who he *is*: the power of his Father at work, healingly and restoringly so. His presence is never an inert and static presence: he is present as One who is at work as One who does his Father's work. E. C. Hoskyns puts it well: 'The works of Jesus have been given Him by the Father to bear witness to the nature of His mission; and they are final, finished and complete acts. That is to say, so far from being experimental and tentative, they make known the final *power of God* [emphasis mine] to forgive sin and to give eternal life to His children.'[13]

Many, however, are taken aback by Jesus' exercise of power. 'Therefore the Jews started persecuting Jesus, because he was doing such things on the Sabbath' (John 5.16). In John 5.19-28 Jesus describes the authority that he has from his Father to heal. He declares to the Jews (as a Jew), 'Very truly, I tell you, the hour is coming, and is now here, when the dead will hear (*akousousin*) the voice of the Son of God, and those who hear (*akousantes*) will live' (John 5.25). What he wants his people to do – and us, too – is to *hear* and to believe him. His own people are subject to scathing critique – in short, judgment – precisely because they do not acknowledge that a new reality has confronted them in this man who is the Son of God. The new reality that is present to them and has confronted them is that this man is not only the author of resurrection but also of judgment. 'In Jesus the world is confronted by the End.'[14] The End is present and contemporary to them in him. The End – that is, Jesus

---

[12] Hoskyns, *Fourth Gospel*, 1:297.

[13] Hoskyns, *Fourth Gospel*, 1:303.

[14] Hoskyns, *Fourth Gospel*, 1:298.

– is present, moreover, to all times, remaking them in accordance with the will of his Father whom he loves. The hour is no less present to the Jews who sought to kill him because he called 'God his own Father, thereby making himself equal to God', than it is to us (John 5.18). We too live in this hour; we too must hear the voice that is speaking to us and live.

This is of course quite difficult for people to appreciate. We are used to and often at home in a world wherein we expect to hear nothing because we already 'know' what is real and what can be. But the joy of hearing Jesus is that we realize the extent to which our time is encroached upon by his time. Indeed, Jesus does speak and in so doing he calls 'into question all the criteria by which – in normal affairs – I [we] judge what is possible, what is reasonable, what is admirable'.[15] As late modern people we find it difficult to believe that the reign of God is present to us and impinging upon us. That is why we must linger with this healing episode. It attests Jesus' mission, which is basically that of expounding God's power, truth and love. It teaches us, furthermore, that we are aligned with his mission to the extent that we hear him and obey. And if we truly hear and obey, we stand within God's final order. We stand as those aligned with the flesh of Jesus. 'The place of decision is the flesh of Jesus, His audible words and His visible death, in fact, the historical event of His mission.'[16] He is the 'place of decision' insofar as he *is* God's judgment upon humankind. And so, he judges the man's illness, deeming it to be incommensurate with his love, with the life he is and gives. More than that, he judges his people's unbelief as he judges this man's illness. Thus the decision that Jesus *is* confronts us now, is present to us now as it confronted and was present to his people then: 'Very truly, I tell you, anyone who hears (*akouōn*) my word and believes (*pisteuōn*) him who sent me has eternal life, and does not come under judgment, but has passed from death to life' (John 5.24).

Healing and Resurrection

Having attended briefly to one of Jesus' healings and the discourse which follows it, it would be good to reflect upon this healing episode in light of the resurrection. This is because the resurrection contemporizes it. That is to say, without attending in a preliminary fashion for a moment to the matter which will occupy us in the fourth chapter

[15] Newbigin, *Exposition*, 69.
[16] Hoskyns, *Fourth Gospel*, 1:300.

– that is, the presence of Christ's love – it would be all too easy to read the Gospel account as an artifact of the past or to regard the activity of the One of whom it speaks as past. But we must not. Indeed, we ought to hear Torrance's wise counsel that it is in the church that the One who acted thus is present. The church is as the place 'filled with his own presence', a presence which makes 'it the place among humanity where his saving acts continue to operate effectively for all who hear and believe in the gospel'. Accordingly, we must gloss the resurrection appearances even now, for it is on their basis that 'his saving acts continue to operate effectively', and that we can even now conceive of him as presently ministering and healing.[17] The Spirit of Christ and of the Father is present, the Spirit as the mode of the risen and ascended Christ's presence, in such a way that creation is able to realize its eschatological relation to God. Following Cyril, the Son and Spirit bear such a close relation to one another that they can be said to be 'not at all different'.[18] This is not to suggest the absence of an eschatological reserve. Rather, it is to suggest that the healing – and the resurrection and ascension as what contemporize it – is indicative of the 'new normal' of which the church is the herald.

The resurrection is the ultimate vindication of the powerful ministry of Christ, the power that is marvelously at work in the healing of the ill man and in our lives and world. However, at first glance, John's account of the resurrection might lead us to think otherwise. For it is, in Newbigin's words, 'calm and unspectacular'. The emphasis in John 20 'is upon the restoration of the personal relationships broken by the events of Friday, upon the way in which Mary of Magdala, the disciples, and Thomas are brought into a new and deeply intimate relationship with Jesus'.[19] The restoration of 'personal relationships', to which Newbigin refers, includes an enabling to faith. Because he is risen, his disciples can believe and share in the Life which is present to them in the flesh as truly life. If this be the case, we can see how his healing and restoration of the ill man anticipates the ultimate restoration of all things, the firstfruits of which are manifest in his resurrection. After the events of Friday and Saturday, the disciples returned to a closed world. It is only the resurrected Jesus' presence and words on Sunday that break it open.

---

[17] Torrance, *Atonement*, 372.

[18] Norman Russell, *Commentary on John's Gospel*, in *Cyril of Alexandria* (London: Routledge, 2000), 123.

[19] Newbigin, *Exposition*, 261.

We see this most poignantly in Jesus' interaction with Mary: 'Jesus said to her, "Mary!"' (John 20.16). John focuses not so much on the empty tomb: that is only the beginning. Rather, it is for John more 'the creation of a new relationship between Jesus and those who believe in him… This new relationship will be mediated by the Spirit whose coming depends upon the completion of Jesus' journey to the Father (John 7.39; 16.7). This is what is now to be made clear.'[20] We, like Jesus' disciples, are invited to live in and from this new relationship to be accepted in faith and mediated by the Spirit. This is what is real. Precisely because it is mediated by the Spirit, this new relationship between Jesus and those who believe in him is a contemporary reality, 'a contemporary news event'.[21] It is a relationship in which Christ by the power of the Spirit continually speaks, graciously interrupting and thus healing our closed world. This is the power at work in his resurrection and ascension. The resurrected One says: 'Receive (*Labete*) the Holy Spirit' (John 20.22). To receive the Spirit is to receive Jesus himself, present in the mode of promise.

To live as those to whom he is present is to 'live in a relationship of love and of obedience to Jesus which nothing can destroy'.[22] When he rises from the dead and breathes the Spirit, he creates a new community which takes up space in the world in the love and obedience of its members. Jesus' new community attests the new reality that is manifested, in this instance in the restoration of personal relations between the Shepherd and the sheep. The one who rules over death called his sheep then and does so now. He is present as One whose ministry is that of gathering, upholding and sending. His call is indeed the basis by which his sheep live. And he calls them as the One who ascends. So says Jesus to Mary: '"I am ascending (*anabebēka*) to my Father and your Father, to my God and your God"' (John 20.17). Hoskyns comments, 'He now declares to Mary, and through her to the disciples, that the time has come for Him to ascend to the Father and therefore for the *inauguration* [emphasis mine] of the new order… The message which she had to deliver was therefore that the new order, the order of the powerful action of the Spirit of God, the New Covenant, was now imminent.'[23]

---

[20] Newbigin, *Exposition*, 265.

[21] Christopher Morse, *The Difference Heaven Makes: Rehearing the Gospel as News* (London: T&T Clark, 2010), 8.

[22] Newbigin, *Exposition*, 266.

[23] Hoskyns, *Fourth Gospel*, 2:647.

Yes, Jesus departs: he is no longer here in the mode of the flesh. And yet, the new order of the Spirit is an order in which he is no less present and active. He is, rather, present and as such active in the Spirit. Note: not as the Spirit but by the Spirit, can he be said to be present.

This new order which is anticipated in Jesus' healing of the ill man is now about to be fully realized. As the risen and soon to be ascended One, the new order – even better, the new reality – *is* present in the powerful action of his Spirit. The new reality is Jesus' (continuing) presence and activity of which the disciples and we are witnesses. This is to say that Jesus, as he was sent by the Father, sends us in sending his disciples. However, he does not send us on a mission to which he is not present and in which he is not wholly at work. He is ever only present now in the Spirit as One who is doing what he did then: that is, gathering, upholding and sending disciples in order to participate in his healing of the nations. We are not to take over from him, from his person and mission, as if he were 'an absent master'.[24] The power demonstrated in the resurrection, ascension and breathing of the Spirit is power that is present in the Spirit to men and women to the end that they can attest the Life that is truly life. By the powerful working of his Spirit they are enabled to go forth as those who live in the light of a very definite presence and who seek to hear their present master – albeit often all too provisionally – and in hearing him, call others to do the same.

An essay about Christ's ongoing presence as One who ministers in accord with the power, truth and love he is, undertaken with a view to its implications for ethics, for our understanding of the ground and space in which we act, must take account of the implications contained in the resurrection appearances of Christ in John's Gospel. The church's mission is to bear witness to the power of God as demonstrated and present in the life, death, resurrection and ascension of Jesus – the latter being inclusive of the breathing of the Spirit. So Newbigin: 'The Church, consecrated in the truth by the promise of the Spirit, is sent into the whole world to be the bearer of that effective action.'[25] Newbigin's point is that the church's mission – to be the bearer of the effective action of God in the world – is not to be regarded as a burden: that is, a realizing on its own of the mission of a person confined to the past. In Torrance's words, 'The

[24] Newbigin, *Exposition*, 269.
[25] Newbigin, *Exposition*, 269.

church is not therefore the extension of the incarnation.'[26] Nor is the
church to be regarded as an extension of a person who is no longer
present. The action of Jesus – the new order of taking away sin, of
healing humankind – is ongoing and presently effective in the Spirit.
He lives. The church bears or witnesses to 'that effective action'. That
his action is effective is indicative of his power to do among us now
what he did then.

Just as 'Jesus came and stood among them and said, "Peace be
with you"' so he too comes and stands among us and says the same
(John 20.19). The gap between the then and there and the here and
now is really not so large. In fact, there is not any gap. 'In the slender
series of New Testament accounts of the disciples' meetings with the
risen Lord we are dealing with attestation of the pure presence of
God. The Easter story actually speaks of a present without any future,
of an eternal presence of God in time.'[27] He is present and speaking
to us now the words he spoke to his first disciples then. John does
not 'separate resurrection, ascension, and the giving of the Spirit in
the way that Luke does' because he 'understands them as – in some
senses – a single event' which is 'present without any future'.[28]

The church's mission – which is not additional to its being – is thus
a mission normed by a single event present in all of its power. Ethics,
too, takes its cues from an event that is past and, precisely because of
the power of the Spirit breathed upon those first disciples and us in
them, also contemporary. In more technical terms, 'Christ assimilates
the church into the new covenant'.[29] That Torrance uses the present
tense is crucial to acknowledge: Christ is present and as One present
he is assimilating the church – despite so many appearances to the
contrary – into the new covenant. The Fourth Gospel is especially
subversive at just this point because it relativizes Lessing's so-called
'ugly ditch' by pointing to Christ as One who continually comes in the
power of the Spirit.[30] How indeed can an unsubstitutable happening
like the resurrection of Jesus be regarded as constitutive of reality?
The scandal of the Christian Gospel is that the empty tomb and resurrection appearances are concrete declarations which bring one into

[26] Torrance, *Atonement*, 369.
[27] *CD* I/2, 114.
[28] Newbigin, *Exposition*, 270; and *CD* I/2, 114.
[29] Torrance, *Atonement*, 368.
[30] 'That is: *accidental truths of history can never become the proof of necessary truths of reason.*' Gotthold Lessing, *Lessing's Theological Writings*, trans. Henry Chadwick (London: A&C Black, 1956), 53, original emphasis.

communion with the new reality. This reality is simply 'an abiding in him as he forever abides in the Father through the presence of the Spirit'.[31] Reality, then, is an event, a movement best responded to in terms of an active abiding. Ethics, actions appropriate to this reality, are actions demonstrative of an abiding in Christ. And in abiding in him, one abides in his Father by the powerful presence of the Spirit – hence ethics is deeply trinitarian in shape.

That the disciples are sent, and, as those who are sent, are breathed upon by the Spirit, is indicative, furthermore, of their need and ours to 'be transformed and recreated by the insufflation of the Holy Spirit'.[32] In a manner which recalls Genesis 2.7, the breathing upon them of the Spirit is indicative of a profoundly 'new creative act of God, a second creation, rather than a repetition of the first creation'.[33] Part of what makes this new is that the Creator-Spirit, understood as the ongoing presence and guarantor of the efficacy of the risen and ascended Jesus' ministry, does not depart from the disciples. This is, as Matthew 28.20 reminds us, an abiding 'to the end of the age'. Indeed, what is so startling about the resurrection appearances in John is just how transparent the disciples' times (and ours in them) are to the risen Lord. 'Although the doors were shut, Jesus came and stood among them and said, "Peace be with you" ' (John 20.26). He is present and as such ministering until he comes again.

The Jesus who stood among them stands among us too. He never departs but rather keeps on standing among us by his Word and Spirit – even so, we pray 'Come, Lord Jesus!' (Rev. 22.20). He does not stand among us as one indifferent to us. Rather, he wills through us to do his ministry. His work – he is always working, invisibly – is ongoing, and never without visible form: it is always expansive. Its present form, for John, is belief. It is effective, too, in that it continually evokes faith on the part of those to whom it is directed. The disciples' mission begins and ends with belief. And right hearing or believing issues in sending. Being sent involves visible participation in what the Lord *is* doing in this the new age of the Spirit. This is 'the age of the Spirit, when Jesus will dwell with his believing people and they with him not by their seeing but by their believing through the word of the apostles (John 17.20)'.[34] Dwelling with them and now us,

---

[31] Newbigin, *Exposition*, 270.

[32] Hoskyns, *Fourth Gospel*, 2:649.

[33] Hoskyns, *Fourth Gospel*, 2:649.

[34] Newbigin, *Exposition*, 272.

he works in us through their word, present as One who calls us into their school to the end that the power demonstrative in his healing of a sick man and most resplendently in his resurrection be at work in us too.

REALITY AND POWER

The Contested Character of Power

Power is, as Steven Lukes states, ' "an essentially contested concept" '.[35] That it is a contested term should not be a surprise. One need only consider the wide variety of the uses of the word in everyday speech. In this connection, Stephen Sykes writes, 'The term is plainly one of a group of words, including violence, force, domination, manipulation, influence, authority, persuasion, and others which the English language has at its disposal for speaking of how agencies, both personal and collective, make a difference in the world.'[36] Sykes's point about power's contested character and of agencies making a difference is important to consider. Indeed, the concern of this section is to describe the immanent and contemporary identity of the Son, and thus the way in which his power at work in his healing ministry is an overflow of the life he is *in se* together with the Father and Spirit. Our task in this section is to give an account of his person, who he is, specifically with a view to the ways in which the *kind* of power at work in his ministry is a display of his immanent life. The reason for doing so is simple: we would be wise not to separate what we have to say about power from the eternality of the Son, and thus the considerable force that the immanent aspects of Christology have not only for ethical imperatives but for an account of his contemporaneity.

Christians believe Christ *is* the centre. Although Christians do not always agree on what that implies, there is widespread consensus that Jesus Christ is the particular agent through whom a unique power – indeed, God's power, the power of the Spirit – is at work in the world. Christians confess this power is not without effect, that it indeed makes all the difference in the world – and for the better. So it is appropriate that the beginning of a section that attempts

---

[35] Steven Lukes, *Power: A Radical View*, 2nd ed. (Basingstoke: Palgrave Macmillan, 2005), quoted in Stephen Sykes, *Power and Christian Theology* (London: T&T Clark, 2006), 7.

[36] Sykes, *Power*, 8.

to map the identity of the One who acts thus in all of his eternality and contemporaneity should acknowledge, rather forthrightly, the contested character of the term power. Such an account should want to be clear that there are many conceptions of power, and that what follows is not an attempt to speak of power in any general sense, but power understood as ingredient in the identity of a particular person who is eternal and as such contemporary in the Spirit. Thus the task in this section is one of describing the 'reality-indication' given by this person in all of his identity as the Son of God become Son of Man.[37]

The first thing that needs to be said is that the kind of power we are talking about, and what difference it makes, is a power that is hardly at our disposal. The identity of this One who acts powerfully to overcome sickness as a manifestation of evil is not as one who is present in such a way that he gives himself entirely over to us. Even in his radical self-abasement on the cross, he remains himself. And so, his power is not a power that can be domesticated and twisted in accord with our own ends, whatever they may be.

The idea that to speak truthfully about a contested notion such as power requires open hands, indeed a receptive spirit as to what true power is, is not often well-received. I suspect this is because we are as late-modern or hyper-modern people conditioned as such – given the contested character of even those terms – to assume that there is not anything beyond ourselves, our conceptions. As Charles Taylor writes, we in the West are secular people, understanding ourselves in terms of ' "closed world structures" '.[38] That is, there is nothing beyond the 'immanent frame'; there is nothing beyond ourselves, and our own exercise of whatever we deem to be power.[39] We are those imprisoned by a world in which God is regarded as absent. But imagine for a moment a different state of affairs. Imagine indeed that our world is permeable, indeed permeated by, One who is present, powerfully ministering.

To imagine the character of this power is to harken to a person beyond ourselves. The work of this person is precisely what gives us our clues as to the kind of power we encounter. The work of

---

[37] The language of 'reality-indication' is taken from John Webster, who writes, 'In an ethical context Christological statements function as reality-indications.' See ' "Where Christ is": Christology and Ethics', in *Christology and Ethics*, ed. F. LeRon Shults and Brent Waters (Grand Rapids, MI: Eerdmans, 2010), 38.

[38] Charles Taylor, *A Secular Age* (Cambridge, MA: Belknap Press of Harvard University Press, 2007), 551.

[39] Taylor, *A Secular Age*, 551.

this person is our reference point, the place at which the many competing and contested accounts of power are measured. Indeed, many are found wanting because they do not correspond to the work of this person. The work of this person is the work of reconciliation. Reconciliation, the chief work of God, is accomplished by God in Christ through the power of the Spirit. Because it is, Christians believe, *God's* work, we do not drown in a sea of indeterminancy as we begin to sketch an account of the eternal identity of the One who is present and powerfully ministering. Power is indeed displayed in the healing of the sick man in John 5.1-18. But it is power exercised for the sake of reconciliation – or better, it is reconciling and, in the Spirit, revealing power.

If our talk and thought about power is to be true, if it is to be disciplined, it is to be referred to 'our reconciliation with God accomplished by God Himself'.[40] This is important to recognize because reconciliation, and the power ingredient in it, is the work of. One beyond ourselves. It does not belong to us and, therefore, is not something that we can manipulate. Reconciliation refers, rather, to a person and work that is alien to us, that invades our reality, thereby making it new. What unique aspect or dimension of our reconciliation is manifest in the healing of the sick man? The healing and the resurrection as the act that contemporizes the healing denote the coming into being of a new world, the declaration of a victory won. The world that comes into being is a world shorn of sin and death. It is a victory over all the forces – personal, societal and cosmic – that mysteriously and altogether absurdly oppose God's good covenantal purposes for his world. In the presence of Jesus, a kind of power is at work that gives life to what is dead, makes alive what was slain.

This power is not something that belongs to the past, as my reading of John 5 and 20 demonstrates, that has to be therefore made relevant for today. Although, as Christians, we seek to live in light of this victory over sin and death, no longer fearing death's curse, we do indeed long for the day when the victory accomplished will become *visible* for all to see. It is very tempting to think about the power at work in the healing of this man as inert, confined to the past; to think of Jesus' healing ministry as One proper to the three years or so of his public ministry. But if the man Jesus who reconciles humanity to himself, whose healing ministry functions as one dimension of this reconciliation, indeed lives, *declaring* and proclaiming himself

---

[40] *CD* II/1, 588.

today, we cannot proceed in the description of power's character without constant recourse to his person which is the ultimate reality-indication.[41] Because the work of his person is constitutive of what is real and true, it is we who need to be in all things laid hold of in order that our thinking, speaking of, and service toward the power of God at work in the life of Jesus be correct. So the task ahead of us is this: to ask after how the immanent life of the Son is the guarantor of his contemporaneity and thus of his continually laying hold of our thinking and speaking about power, of our acting in accord with God's power. His person in its eternality and therefore contemporaneity is what renders power less contested and more transparent to its true source, and ongoingly effective.

Jesus' healing declares the will of the God of Israel, one who will not let even the death of his own Son interrupt his good purposes for his beloved people. God's will is that we be his people, which is precisely what follows from his eternal decision or determination to be our God.[42] If such is the case, two points follow regarding his identity as seen at work in his ministry. First, we are not dealing with a nominalist understanding of power. Hermann Bavinck defines such a view as follows: 'The nominalists defined the omnipotence of God not only as his power to do whatever he will, but also as his power to will anything.'[43] The presence of God's power at work in the healing episodes of John 5 is not nearly so indeterminate. God does not will anything, but rather one thing, which is disclosive of who God is: reconciliation. The power at work in the healing ministry of Jesus is unitive power. It unites not only human beings to God, overcoming the verdict, the seemingly definite No humanity pronounced upon him by crucifying his Son; in the place of the No, there also stands the declaration which overcomes: 'you are mine'. Sin's noetic and ontic effects are thereby eliminated. A simple physical healing, while not to be understood as reconciliation in the Pauline sense of the term, is nonetheless identical with a feature of it. I am thinking especially of Paul's portrait of the 'cosmic' Christ, the Christ of Ephesians and Colossians. As 'the firstborn (*prōtotokos*) from the dead', he is the new creation; he is reconciliation. He is this

---

[41] 'His [Christ's] prophecy is the direct self-declaration of His life of grace and salvation, of the life of the God who has descended to man and of the man exalted to God.' See *CD* IV/3, 52.

[42] See 2 Cor. 6.16; Ezek. 37.27.

[43] Herman Bavinck, *Reformed Dogmatics*, trans. John Vriend, vol. 2, *God and Creation* (Grand Rapids, MI: Baker Academic, 2004), 247.

as One who 'might come to have first place in everything (*en pasin*)' (Col. 1.18). The sick man's healing is indicative of Jesus' identity as One who wills to be first, and so displaces what prevents him from having 'first place in everything', including the unnamed man's illness and the unbelief of his people.

Second, and equally problematic, would be the opposite of the nominalist view, namely the idea 'that God can do only what he wills and nothing that he does not will... God has fully exhausted his power in the existing world'.[44] To assume so is to suggest a rather odd view of the relationship between God and his will. That God, for example, acts in raising Jesus from the dead through the power of the Spirit is not at all an exhaustion of God's power but rather its most eloquent display. God is not somehow imprisoned by his will, for his will is, as Bavinck states, 'identical with his being'.[45] That God has acted in the way he has in the person of Christ is fully disclosive of who God is: there is not 'another' God behind Jesus of Nazareth. The presence of Christ – a presence that does not will the sick man to be as he is – discloses the being of God. God in the person of Christ comes among us as One present in power. Accordingly, there is not an uneasy or ambiguous relationship between God and his will – what God wills is really truly revelatory of who he is. Knowledge of God is knowledge of his will.

We ought to say more, however, about Christ's person, which functions as *the* reality-indication. For it is this person, his life, death, resurrection and ascension, that is the center of reality. Accordingly, I think it wise to talk about reconciliation and the person of Jesus in the same sentence, for Jesus' identity is as the reconciler; he is present as the reconciler ministering the reconciliation he is. He effects reconciliation as reconciliation just is what he is. And reconciliation applies to every moment of his life. He is present as reconciliation for he effects what he is. This is what grounds an account of the real. The identity of Christ as reconciliation bespeaks his presence as reconciliation, and so effects among us what he is and reveals: reconciliation. Barth writes,

> It is from this centre [Christ] that He [God] sees and conditions, elects and calls, exercises grace and judgment. It is from this centre that He loves the world. For He Himself is in the centre. This centre is His omnipotent Word by which He created and governs and upholds the world, withstands its rebellion

[44] Bavinck, *God and Creation*, 247.
[45] Bavinck, *God and Creation*, 247.

and restores it to Himself, not only calling it back from all sides, but *omnipotently* [emphasis mine] bringing it back to peace with Himself.[46]

These very dense sentences warrant explanation. At the centre of an account of reconciliation is the Word. This is not a general kind of Word, but an omnipotent Word – the Word that heals the sick man and breathes the Spirit. The Word's omnipotence is shown forth not only by his work of creating, governing and upholding the world, but also by his activity in bringing it back to himself. God the Father exercises his agency in the world through the Word. His creation, governance and upholding is truly omnipotent in the Word, despite its being confronted with mass rebellion.

We are a part of that rebellion inasmuch as we resist the *presence* of God's power in Christ: indeed, we often resist any other resources than our own. This is just what fallen people do. But our rebellion – thanks be to God – is re-contextualized, situated in light of the order and action of Another. That is one of the primary functions of the healing episodes in the Gospels. The presence of illness and unbelief on the part of his people cannot withstand his ministering presence, he who *is* God's omnipotent Word. He puts to death our faithlessness by his faithful life, our sin by his crucifixion, and is vindicated by his resurrection, enabling us to pray in him in accord with his identity as the ascended One whose heavenly session is his ongoing work of bringing the world back to peace with himself. In short, reconciliation is new creation. In Torrance's words, 'He comes to be God for man in order to remake man for God'.[47] Ingredient in this remaking is the healing of our bodies. The omnipotence of the Word is indeed omnipotent to restore, to re-unite, to re-create and convert. The result is peace. And the peace that has been established *is* reality. The power at work in this person, the person of Christ, is the power to restore, the once for all announcement that the world has been brought to the peace that 'surpasses all understanding' (Phil. 4.7).

Ethics must assiduously attend to Jesus' self-proclamation and thus to what he actually does. Ethics is indeed simply 'the disciplined habit of thinking and acting in Christ'.[48] Christ Jesus is a person who is active. Because he rose, he lives and is present today, and his work is

---

[46] *CD* II/1, 605.

[47] Thomas F. Torrance, *Incarnation: The Person and Life of Christ*, ed. Robert T. Walker (Downers Grove, IL: IVP Academic, 2008), 109.

[48] Torrance, *Incarnation*, 376.

'immediately effective' in the power of the Spirit.[49] Power, therefore, is not a concept but a person; it is a descriptive gloss particular to the way in which he enacts his identity and ministers as the One he is. It is that which God does in the person of Jesus by not only restoring Jesus to communion with himself in the Spirit by raising him from the dead, but in so doing restoring us too. When one then describes the power ingredient in this particular person, a profoundly different account emerges which makes all the difference for the true will to power in persons, societies and even the cosmos. In the person of Christ, the omnipotent will of God is manifest. His identity is as One who is God's will to heal and save. God's will is Christ.

To know Jesus is to know God's power: the power of Father and Son *is* identical. Moreover, to know Jesus is to know what God omnipotently knows and wills. That is to say, there is no knowledge of God's will and power outside the knowledge of Jesus Christ, his life, cross and resurrection. God's knowing, over against nominalism and its antithesis, is thus not a matter of him having the power to will whatever he wills. Knowledge is identical to an act, a person, and so too is God's will. What God knows and wills for *all* is the person of Jesus Christ, to live *in* and act *on* the basis of the present ministry of Christ. If this point not be emphasized, we are again left in a sea of indeterminancy regarding the dogmatic location of ethics.

The Power of the Immanent Son

In meeting God's power, the power at work in Christ, one encounters God's knowing and willing, the grain of the universe. Power is never to be isolated from a determination – namely, that of peace with God himself. It is this determination which is *the* reality-indication ingredient in the person of Christ. What we learn in Scripture about this determination or will is that it is an omnipotent determination which withstands the world's rebellion. That humanity – the life of all humankind – is made over and new in Christ is just what the hypostatic union accomplishes. But he can and does do this – as the person he is – because he is eternal.

If the movement in ethics ought always to be from God to humanity, inclusive as it is of the movement of humanity to God, one must take a moment to reflect upon the eternal basis of such a movement. To talk about the eternality of Christ as what grounds his always 'working' matters precisely because without such an

[49] Hoskyns, *Fourth Gospel*, 1:294.

account we risk talking about the presence of Christ in purely interventionist terms (John 5.17). The power of this One as the presence of God's power 'working' is his immanent life. That is not to take away from the unsubstitutable character of these accounts, but it is to say that we are not beholding in them a reaction. Instead, in the Gospels, we are witnesses to the enactment of an eternal determination: that 'all things have been created…for him' (Col. 1.16). It is the Son of God's eternal determination which is manifest here: the eternal determination of Son and Father to guarantee for the creature their participation as creatures in the blessings of covenant fellowship with themselves. To be sure, the way in which this eternal purpose is realized is shaped by the fact that we have sinned. But our sin and its fruits do not determine God's will. God's will – indicative as it is of God's being – is to humanize. The surety of the reconciliation Jesus is, enacts and reveals is rooted in his person as the eternal Son. An account of the eternality or immanent life of the Son whose ministering presence in Jesus Christ effectively confronts illness is thus necessary if the divine character of the work be granted. Without it, the Gospels can be read only as interventions, not descriptions of the grain of the universe which is the outworking in time of the life of the trinity, specifically the life of the eternal Son.

So in describing this determination – which is also at the same time the economic act(s) of a person – we are describing reality, an omnipotent reality rooted in an immanent identity: 'I am the resurrection and the life' (John 10.10). And it is at this point that we can begin to offer a modest correction to Sykes's description. In talking about the power at work in the healing ministry of Jesus effective now in the power of the Spirit, we are not only speaking of a power that 'make[s] a difference in the world'.[50] Rather, we are pointing to a power that *establishes* the world as well. Again: 'My Father is still working and I am also working' (John 5.17). The power at work in the person of Jesus, his ministry, does far more than heal: indeed, inasmuch as it creates, governs and upholds, it is demonstrative once again of an eternal determination regarding what is and is to be. When individuals and communities find themselves grasped by what *is*, they will hear the omnipotent Word, the very center, who '*constitutes* creaturely reality by binding it into his own'.[51]

[50] Sykes, *Power*, 8.
[51] Webster, ' "Where Christ Is",' in *Christology and Ethics*, 50, original emphasis.

By defining power with reference to this person, specifically his presence and thus ministry as the triumph over all opposition to God's covenantal purposes manifest proleptically in the healing of the sick man and ultimately in Jesus' resurrection, and in arguing that this is indicative of reality, we see that an account of the immanent life of the Son has considerable moral force. That he always is life together with his Father and the Spirit whom he receives and breathes means that nothing even short of his own death can prevent him, together with the Father and Spirit, from accomplishing who he eternally is amongst us and for us. Because the power at work that makes each and every day a gift is not ours to possess or handle, we can begin to recognize that our power – or, our sinful will to power – has been broken in accord with the grain of the universe. So Lehmann: 'The will to power has been transformed into the power to will what God wills by the power of God's Messiah.'[52] This need not imply disaster for an account of human agency. Indeed, the *criterion* of the true will for power is simply whether we can live with the breaking of our will: in the case of the sick man, his willingness to testify before the Jews that it 'was Jesus who had made him well' (John 5.18). The power at work in the resurrected and ascended person of Jesus who breathes the Spirit is present, very present, not waiting to be realized, but ready to break the sinful will to power. That we learn to live in alignment with the presence of this power which continually breaks our will, and in doing so humanizes it, might just make all the difference for who we are and how we live.

The True Exercise of Power

This is a new possibility, if you will, which comes to us from outside, from the identity of Christ as the presence among us of the omnipotent power of God: omnipotent to reconcile. Its guarantor is the love of Jesus Christ. It is he who is and brings the crisis to our will for power. The language of crisis is crucial, because it reminds us of the degree to which this power *is* in the Spirit present and ministering. Our multifold exercises of power – so many of them dehumanizing – are subject to the withering crisis caused by a different exercise of power which wills to render our exercise correspondent to itself, inasmuch as we are able to live with the breaking of our will for power. Without this emphasis, it would be all too easy to treat the power of God at work in the (healing) ministry of Jesus as once again a relic,

---

[52] Lehmann, *Ethics*, 97.

as something that we need to carry forward today into new contexts unaware of or indifferent to it. Similarly, it would be 'reasonable' to view the power manifest in Jesus' ministry as a kind of divine response to circumstances unforeseen rather than the display of One whose identity is eternal and immanent, together with the Father and Spirit. And so, the person who is power is not ours to control, but rather is one to whom we are to be conformed, for in giving us a share in his power through the Spirit who interprets it to us, we are not only simply interrupted by him but also established in him. He is present through the power of the Spirit as One constitutive of reality; the power present and at work in individuals, the church and the world is the power of the present Jesus. To live in accordance with his ongoing breaking of our will to power is to flourish, to reflect as creatures the One who was, is and will be.

One of the most important implications of the establishment of the *crisis* that is his person concerns its non-competitive character. That is, we need not conceive of the presence of such power as present in the ministry of this person that breaks our will to power, as a power that destroys the legitimate exercise of creaturely power. The power at work in the ministry of Jesus, the power of God's love that reconciles and sends us forth to tell others of the One who makes well, does not threaten the exercise of human power *per se*. In Barth's words,

> [The creature] will never jealously oppose its own power to this [God's] power, but rather place it at its disposal, in the knowledge that it already belongs to the divine love even before it has decided to put its power at its disposal, and that it can decide to do so only because the divine power has itself disposed concerning its power.[53]

Two things follow from Barth's statement. First, whether we realize it or not, our purported power is already ruled over by God's divine power. That is, our power is always already circumscribed by another power, the power of God's love, which sanctifies. There is a reality which lies outside of us – *reconciliation* – to which we belong, every one of us. Such is the nature of creaturely reality understood in accord with the hypostatic union: it seeks and finds those who have not sought it out. The Son of God by the Spirit unites human essence to himself. Second, reality binds us to itself; it is living and active, presiding over and remaking our use of the power appropriate to us as creatures. Reality impinges, in other words, in order to heal. But the reality of the power of God's love does not denigrate our exercise

---

[53] *CD* II/1, 599.

of power or nullify it *per se*; however, it does encroach upon it and therefore oblige. Reality obliges inasmuch as it conforms us to itself, and so continues its ongoing healing and forgiving work.

What is more, in arguing that power 'belongs to the divine love', we see the end to which our exercise of power as creatures is to be disposed. Just as God's power present in the person of Jesus is the power to bring the world back to peace with himself, so too is our power to reflect or correspond to such an exercise of power. The power of the resurrected one which declares God's Yes, which announces the forgiveness of sins and saves from death, is power that takes shape in and among us by the Holy Spirit, enabling us to share in the possibilities ingredient in the presence of a different kind of power, the power present in the contemporary ministry of Jesus Christ. Indeed, the task of ethics is to act so as to be transparent to and thus to participate in this power.

This is an important point, for the reason that the power of God displayed in the person of Jesus – him whose words bring about that of which they speak – is not a power that causes creatures to forsake their responsibility and thus to misuse freedom. Indeed, the Father in Christ forgives sin and saves from death. Jesus' resurrection is declarative of this; but the power of God at work in Christ's ministry, power that makes all things new, is not the kind of power that *instantaneously* delivers us from our personal and societal messes. The conflict continues even now. This essay, as a Christological intervention, is also an eschatological one. Eschatological doctrine reminds us, following Torrance, that 'the Kingdom of God now realized intensively in temporal and historical encounter, *in Christ and his encounter with people*, will be realized extensively in a new heaven and earth'.[54]

The intensive and extensive character of the Kingdom gives and offers important insight into the presence of Christ's power. Even as his presence in John 5 is of an extraordinary effect, it is not a presence that is entirely unveiled. His presence is prophetic. As testimony of this, his detractors among his own people are allowed to do just that: detract. But when the hour comes, there will not be room for detraction, for the evil that is an unwillingness to hear. This is because the presence of Christ's power will be apocalyptically present. Accordingly, Christ's presence and its power on the last day will not be like it is now. 'The hour is coming when all those who are in their graves will hear (*akousousin*) his voice', and

---

[54] Torrance, *Atonement*, 404, original emphasis.

rise to either the resurrection of life or of condemnation (John 5.28). One might say that God's will – a forgiving and delivering will – is at the same time inclusive of a certain permission, the permitting – for a time – of sin and its firstfruits death. That ethical inquiry's chief object of concern is God's good will, should cause us to consider seriously that this good will permits for a time, even as it has already destroyed for all time in the person of Jesus, evil. The future to which God calls us has none of this, that is, sin and death; and so the basis of our future hope is nothing other than the prayer 'Come, Lord Jesus' (Rev. 21.20). His coming is the public – or better, apocalyptic – manifestation of his vanquishment of all that is not consistent with the new creation become manifest, of what he in his ministry heralds.

The description offered here of power, inflected in light of what *is*, in accord with Christ's person as eternal and contemporary, is not one that seeks flight from contingency. For Christian faith, contingency is not the enemy. God in Christ, now present through Word and Spirit, is thus present and ministering in a very definite sense as the perfecting power manifest in his resurrection. God wills, via the Holy Spirit, that our actualities be accountable to Christ who is forgivingly, savingly and transformingly present to them. The Spirit of the risen Christ is present as the power of the Christ who has acted and acts *thus*. Accordingly, Jesus' power is *not* threatened by oppressive rule and self-aggrandizing mastery by ears that do not hear. Indeed, as Daniel Migliore writes, 'Jesus refuses to invoke the power of God in a way that would merely support the dominant and dehumanizing ideas of divine and human power.'[55] Were he to do so, he would violate his will which includes a permission of evil for a time, and merely underwrite those powers that seek to have their way by coercion, rather than by conformity to the power at work in the acts that splendidly declare that the days of those powers are profoundly limited and numbered. They will be judged and so raised 'to the resurrection of condemnation'. The true exercise of power is a matter of doing good, and so of being raised 'to the resurrection of life' (John 5.29).

---

[55] Daniel L. Migliore, *The Power of God and the Gods of Power* (Louisville, KY: Westminster John Knox, 2008), 52.

THE COMMAND OF POWER

The Command of the Omnipotent Word

It is now time to think in very concrete terms about the manner in which the present and ministering Christ implicates us in his presence in the form of a command – a 'Do this'. Having offered an account of the eternal identity of Jesus Christ as what secures an account of his contemporaneity, I shall describe Christ's presence as the law of creaturely being. In the previous section, I described the eternal and contemporary identity of Christ as concerns John 5. I now want to develop an account of the present ministry of Christ as that which is the 'law' of creaturely being. A more technical way of making the same point would be to say the *is* – reality, Christ's identity as presently ministering – includes a 'thou shalt'. What I sketch in this section is an account of the shape of the 'Do this' – the law – that is generated by an account of reality as disclosed in the ministry of Jesus.

The ongoing presence of Christ *is* a law, a law that makes itself heard and obeyed among men and women, inasmuch as we are given a share through the Spirit in his obedient humanity. The hearing of that law – namely, the honoring of him – effects a particular form of life, namely the life of belief. 'And the Father who sent me has himself testified on my behalf. You have never heard (*akēkoate*) his voice or seen his form, and you do not have his word abiding in you, because you do not believe him whom he has sent (*apesteilen*)' (John 5.37-38). Belief is indeed the thing that is commanded for us in relationship to the one thing in which our life consists. This is to say that the presence of Christ's power is purposive inasmuch as it renders women and men transparent and present to itself.

Another way to state this is to say that this person as he presents himself is also a command; his identity is *imperatival* in character. 'We are God's in Jesus Christ. We are therefore and thereby bound to our neighbour.'[56] He binds us, specifically, to what he is now doing, to his ministry. In other words, he claims us. He claims us for faith, for knowing his Father and for transparency to what his Father in him by the Spirit is now achieving. His own people cannot possibly be a neighbor to the man whose mat is taken up, for they do not

---

[56] Karl Barth, *The Knowledge of God and The Service of God According to the Teaching of the Reformation: Recalling the Scottish Confession of 1560*, trans. J. L. M. Haire and Ian Henderson (Eugene, OR: Wipf and Stock, 2005), 133.

hear Moses' words. The Jews tell the man that it is unlawful to carry
the mat on the Sabbath. But the law of Moses, argues Christ, is a
law that binds one to the neighbor for its content is Christ – 'for he
wrote about me' (John 5.46). Christ claims us by commanding us to
love one another, and so bring glory to his Father. In an arresting
statement, Barth writes, 'Jesus Christ, by making us free, binds us to
God and man. As God's Son He binds us to God, and as Mary's son,
born in the manger and crucified on the Cross, He binds us to man.
This is the claim, twofold but indivisible, which is laid upon us. The
Law, the rule and the first principles underlying all service of God
are – *Jesus Christ*.'[57] This is the Christological basis of ethics, its very
rootedness in the hypostatic union. And any talk of the ethics appropriate to Christ's identity and present ministry is to grasp that his
presence functions as law, as an imperative soaked in grace.

It is tempting to think of the command to believe as burdensome.
After all, it is hard for us to think that law might actually mean
something good for us, for late modern western society is intent on
fleeing from authority. It is hard for us then to conceive of an authority
that is or could be life-giving. Part of the renewal of our minds that
needs to take place is that we learn to recognize that *law* in Christian
thinking is not an oppressive entity or category.[58] However, we tend to
resist the notion that the Gospel claims us precisely because we value
and prize our autonomy above all else. What if the claim of God were
indeed salutary? What if the call or command to believe is a call or
command of *grace*? What if an account of what we are to do on the
basis of Christ's presence were nothing but good news? What if the
'Do this' ingredient in his personhood were as deeply rooted in grace
as the manifestation of the power that heals a man and so anticipates
the apocalyptic unveiling when all things will be made new?

We do not need by our activity – principally belief – to extend the
power at work in Jesus' ministry into the present or try to make it
relevant to our contexts. 'This is because the question of Christian
ethics itself remains malformed unless and until set firmly within a
wider acknowledgement that "God has founded the church beyond
religion and beyond ethics" by the graciously vicarious fulfillment of
the law in the person of the savior.'[59] Ethics is to be taken up in light

[57] Barth, *Knowledge and Service of God*, 135.

[58] See Rom. 12.1-2.

[59] Philip G. Ziegler, ' "Not to Abolish but to Fulfill": The Person of the Preacher and
the Sermon on the Mount', *Studies in Christian Ethics* 22.3 (2009): 288; and Dietrich

of the person of the Son as subjectivized in us through the work of the Spirit. That is, law or command does not describe resources for conduct internal to the self or of the Christian community, a story, or various pressing contingencies or contexts. Rather, ethics understood Christologically is a *destabilized* ethics. It is destabilized precisely because it is an inherently revelational undertaking. What is given in Christ – the fulfillment of Moses' law – 'subjectively takes shape in the mind of the church through the unique enshrining of Christ's gospel'.[60] Ethics understood theologically is thus a destabilized or ever relativized ethics because it is not a matter of implementing a moral program of sorts, but rather a question of being formed by the One – by the objective Person – who truly fulfills himself in us via his faith. By believing in his fulfillment of his will, we too are made participants in him who claims us for *faith*. And his life – his faith, what he is doing, his present ministry – is done into us. Most importantly, we do not then live as those in a kind of vacuum of our own making. Instead, our life is formed by Jesus who is present in the Spirit's power to us, whose present ministry claims us, so that we too might fulfill the law of our being by believing.

Fulfillment of the law of Christ – which is the *telos* of ethics – is possible because the power at work in the ministry of Jesus is really present even as its advent presence is yet to come in such a way that we can be people of our baptism, people to and for whom the risen Jesus is present and welcome in the Spirit. True creatureliness or true humanity is indeed a claimed humanity. It is humanity caught up in a dynamic temporal movement – the movement of the Son of God to us and of us to his Father in him by the power of the Spirit. God identifies himself in Jesus' ministry – to say nothing of his raising him from the dead – as a God who is extraordinarily humanizing. The presence of God's power in Christ is a power that claims men and women so that they can attest it well through acts that point to the basic truth that ears that do not hear – emblematic as they are of sin and death – are on a leash, that they have been reigned in and defeated through the person and (ongoing) ministry of Jesus. Ethics is indeed a matter of being formed by the presence of the Christ, 'the judge of all the ages, [who] is actively present among

Bonhoeffer, 'Protestantism without Reformation', in *No Rusty Swords: Letters, Lectures and Notes, 1928–1936* (London: Collins, 1965), 117.

[60] Torrance, *Atonement*, 330.

humanity'.[61] Indeed, his identity as enacted in the economy of grace is an expansive and inclusive one. He is present to us and contemporary with us as he was to the sick man and to his fellow Jews, even those who excoriated him for his action on behalf of all people. This is to the end that we might believe in him and live.

The same person, the same reality, underlies both the previous section and the current section of this chapter. It is his identity and the acts that constitute his identity which are disclosive of his powerful presence 'in the midst of his people on earth and in history'.[62] His ministry (and passion, resurrection, ascension and session) is definitive of what *is*. But what *is*, includes an *ought*. His person is the basis of the 'Do this', and also in the Spirit the very possibility of our being able to do the 'Do this'. His person is very simply law: it is personhood that implicates. If such is the case, then, the 'Do this' ingredient in the healing episodes is not that we try to heal as Jesus did, to tell the lame and sick to take up their mat. The signs of Jesus' ministry – of which this episode is one, the theme of the Fourth Gospel being new creation – are tremendously self-effacing. Their *telos* is belief. Jesus does these things in order that we, together with his interlocutors, might believe. Those who have the word of Jesus' Father in them are those who 'believe him [Jesus Christ] whom he [the Father] sent'.[63] The appropriate anthropological correlate is again very simply faith.

The divine law is Jesus Christ. He in his ministry enacts not only a kind of power that fundamentally calls into question what we think power is and how it should be exercised, but one that is also the very foundation of power's radical new exercise for which he claims and to which he summons men and women. So he not only precedes us, in that we look to his relinquishment of power at the height of his exercise of power that leads to death. Moreover, we look at how Jesus' relinquishment was vindicated by the same power at work in it, the power of God the Father acting in concert with the Spirit to raise him from the dead. And as One who precedes, he is One who is *present* and also as One whose advent presence is yet to be manifested. As the present one he forms us by or conforms us to his fulfillment of the command to believe. In Torrance's words, 'In the New Testament gospel Christ's faith, his obedience, his knowledge are the foundation of my faith, obedience and knowledge, so that my faith, obedience

---

[61] Torrance, *Atonement*, 428.
[62] Torrance, *Atonement*, 431.
[63] John 5.28.

and knowledge are objectively controlled by his.'[64] The present Christ is ministering so as to create faith *ex nihilo*, the law of creaturely being.

That the one whose identity as the faithful One is present fulfilling the command to believe, and that his presence capacitates faith in the Spirit, is the basis for a more robust account of being human. True human agency is agency whose center lies in Another. 'Very truly, I tell you, the Son can do nothing on his own, but only what he sees the Father doing' (John 5.15). Sinners that we are, we think it good to be transparent to our whims and fancies. The notion that to be fully ourselves is to do nothing on our own, but only to do what the Son does is absurd. The mystery of the Gospel is such that we are incorporated by our baptism into Christ in such a way that we are 'objectively controlled' by him.[65] Rather than that being the end of us, however, it is the beginning. It is life eternal. Paul puts it this way: 'May I never boast of anything except the cross of our Lord Jesus Christ, by which the world has been crucified to me, and I to the world' (Gal. 6.14). The old world is the world that does not believe. But the new world does believe, which is precisely the 'will of him who sent me' (John 5.30).

Immanence and Command

Another way of getting at the character of the way in which the present Christ is law would be to refer to the relationship between the *immanent* life of the Son and the *economic* life of the Son. This might seem an unusual thing to do in the section of a chapter which reflects on the commanding character of Jesus' presence; but it should not really be a surprise. This is because we are conditioned to think that God's self-communication, God's gift of himself in the life, death, resurrection and ascension of Jesus in fulfillment of the promises made to Israel, is *not* the gift of a God who *in se* has life, and is the fullness of life, life eternal. It is important, therefore, that we recognize that God's having acted, as God indeed has, is the highest demonstration of God's freedom to be the One he is – Father, Son and Spirit – even in the face of the most profound threats against himself: unbelief and its firstfruits, namely crucifixion. Consideration of the human 'no' emergent in Jesus' ministry is important, then, precisely because we emerge with a better sense of the extent to which Jesus' ministry is, in Jüngel's difficult word, 'reiteration' of

[64] Torrance, *Incarnation*, 28.
[65] Torrance, *Incarnation*, 28.

his eternal identity as the Son of the Father.[66] Indeed, the Father's determination to 'show him [the Son] even greater works than these' is a determination that is identical to who God *is* (John 5.20). God's having acted healingly so as to elicit belief as God is demonstrative of who he *is*. Again, description of the immanent life of God has considerable moral force. This is the unity of act and being in God. God is life, so naturally God gives life and issues judgements that are in accord with life. It is important that ethics takes seriously that the reality upon which it is founded and the reality to which it is to be continually formed has life in and of itself. God just *is* life and so gives life.

It follows, moreover, that revelation, the history of Israel fulfilled in Jesus, that God is *this* one, does not exhaust God or cause God to become more God. Rather, the language of 'reiteration' points to God's sheer plentitude, and to the truth that what God does, namely act healingly in the Son, is not somehow necessary to God, but rather a profound demonstration of God's freedom to be, in the person of his Son, himself even in the midst of the profoundest depth of creaturely resistance. That resistance will of course culminate on the cross. But it is no doubt present here among his people who even now do not believe Moses and so do not believe in him. This is an important point to acknowledge, precisely because the 'Do this', the call to believe, the basis of which is Jesus Christ, is grounded in God's ontological self-sufficiency. Our acts of faith in relation to God and God's world do not then render reality more real. If reality is indeed God's presence achieving healing in the ministry of the Son in the power of Spirit, then it cannot by us be rendered more complete than it is. The only appropriate thing to do is believe and to act in Christ in a way that corresponds to his ongoing activity, and anticipates his advent presence.

Stated somewhat differently, talk about the asymmetrical and irreversible relationship between the immanent life of God and the economic life of God matters for ethics, precisely because the law of Christ which claims us for faith is grounded in God's own life and is his purpose which is expressive of that life. Webster writes, 'That law is historical and practical, because creatures are temporal agents; but it is "metaphysical", because its grounds lie in the eternal plentitude

[66] See Eberhard Jüngel, *God's Being is in Becoming: The Trinitarian Being of God in the Theology of Karl Barth*, trans. John Webster (Grand Rapids, MI: Eerdmans, 2001), 104–23.

of God's own life and steadfastness of his purpose.'[67] That God wills things to be a certain way – that we accept and believe in the One who has come in his name – is the reflection of a determination which corresponds to the way things are. Inasmuch as we believe, we too become those who live in agreement with an eternal determination, and thus more closely approximate to who we were created to be. It is by God's own doing we become who we are: his children. That we, day in and day out, need to become more correspondent to who we truly are, points to the extent to which we are not God, God who always acts in accordance with who he as Father, Son and Holy Spirit eternally is. So if ethics remains hesitant to account for who he eternally *is*, it follows naturally that its account of what we are to do in him will be impoverished. For it will have moved far too quickly to the 'Do this', having inadequately attended to whether the 'Do this' actually brings us into correspondence with how things really are, or whether it is a 'Do this' which assumes that we have sole responsibility for how things are supposed to be.

We are those called to be, in St. Paul's words, 'imitators (*mimētai*) of God' (Eph. 5.1). We can indeed imitate inasmuch as we believe in the Father and in the Son who raises the dead and in the Spirit whom the Son breathes. It is crucial to note that belief in John's Gospel – the work we are to do – is also the 'good' we are to do. Jesus' words – 'those who have done good to the resurrection of life' (John 5.29) – fit rather well with Paul. To do good is simply to believe, just as Paul characterizes life in the Spirit as a doing of good. In the parenetic portion of his letter to the Galatians, he writes: 'So let us not grow weary in doing what is right, for we will reap at harvest-time, if we do not give up. So then, whenever we have an opportunity, let us work for the good of all, and especially for those of the family of faith' (Gal. 6.9-10). That the power present in Jesus' ministry is therefore at work vivifying us too, as we seek to be formed, and that Jesus' fulfillment of the law is at work in us and impinging upon us through the work of the Spirit amidst us, are testimony once again to the interrelatedness of Christology, pneumatology and ethics. Only when we seriously attend to what is, the person and presence of Christ, will that which we are to do become clear. Indeed, to know what we are to do – good, which is the firstfruits of faith – is to look to One who

---

[67] John Webster, review of *Wie Geschöfe Leben: Some Dogmatic Reflections*, by Hans Ulrich, *Studies in Christian Ethics* 20.2 (2007): 285.

although withdrawn from visible history directs us, as ascended Lord, to the Gospel story 'as the only locus where he may be contacted'.[68]

The Gospel is our law; his presence implicates. Stated differently, the ascended and advent Jesus directs us to his historical existence to discover what we are to do in him. In the case of our text, John 5, it is to believe and thus to do good. This is the form of our participation in his healing ministry: not that we do good in order to establish what is, but that we do the good precisely because what *is* has been announced in the ministry of Jesus and declared effective in his resurrection. 'Jesus Christ Himself, as true God and true man is the Divine *Law* to which we are subject... [and] He, as true God and true man, is also the *fulfillment* of the Law.'[69] He believes and does good so that his belief and doing of good might be fulfilled and find an echo in us.

And so Jesus is not only the living rule for ethics: he himself fulfills the rule he proclaims and attests, coterminous as it is with his presence. 'He was at once the complete revelation of God to man and the perfect correspondence of man's part to revelation.'[70] Christian action in the world is therefore liberated action, precisely because it is action licensed by Jesus as taking place *in* him. Faith recognizes that Jesus indeed interposes himself between the 'Do this' and his followers. That is, Jesus not only asks his followers to live so as to believe that he gives life to things that are naught, but also, as he himself, is the One who accomplishes for us in the Spirit the faith and good he commands. So his ministry is not only demonstrative or revelatory of the humanizing power of the Gospel, but Jesus also, in being resurrected from the dead, effects as the ascended One his presence as the power of God among us through the gift of faith. 'God not only fulfils his promise of love in the covenant in giving himself to humanity in complete and utter grace, but he *accomplishes* for man, and from within man, man's fulfillment of the covenant, man's appropriation of God's gift of himself.'[71] What Torrance suggests is that the ministry of faith is something Jesus, as true God and true man, accomplishes for us. In turning to us he sets us free to live in corresponding fashion to his personhood, as he works out in

---

[68] Torrance, *Atonement*, 431.

[69] Barth, *Knowledge and Service of God*, 141.

[70] Torrance, *Incarnation*, 126.

[71] Torrance, *Incarnation*, 56.

us the exercise of his power for the sake of life through the gracious working of his will.

It is not only God's revelation of true power in the ministry of Christ that matters for power's exercise among creatures, but it is also and equally importantly God in Christ's accomplishment of true power. That we are sinners who do not fulfill our covenantal obligations and responsibilities – in our case, the exercise of faith and the doing of good as the form of service to God and neighbor – does not mean that our efforts to act in accordance with true power are futile. By no means. It is to say that ethics, in particular the exercise of faith, does not take place in a vacuum but *in* Christ. Paul's famous and radical dictum 'in Christ' is quite relevant for our discussion here. It points to the simple truth that Jesus *interposes* himself between himself and his followers. More technically, the person of Christ as mediator, the mediatorship of Christ, matters profoundly for ethics. He not only directs us in a certain way, but upholds us in the Spirit in that very way. He directs to faith and upholds in faith. He is the Yes of God to the No of our unbelief, the Gift of God which overcomes and negates our rejection of God, the One who at the same time accomplishes his person in us and thus what he commands of us. He is 'man's fulfillment of the covenant'.[72] That Barth uses the present tense in describing his mediatorial activity is significant, precisely because it points to his ongoing priestly work – his session – on our behalf. If Christian ethics is indeed situated within a movement, the movement of God to us and of us to God in Christ, then doctrines like the person of the mediator cannot be an afterthought. Ethics as a discipline needs to think after and according to its own foundation in Christ.

Our exercise of faith is thus in accordance with the demonstration of true power. As such it is something that is always truly fulfilled in relation to Another. This Other *is* present – his historical life having been eternally vindicated by his resurrection. He is present 'in the midst of his people on earth and in history' as he who intervenes and is between himself and the law that he is and gives.[73] The law is, again, never a threat but a gift. That his words to his interlocutors transcend their occasionality, that he speaks to us through them in order that we too may have the love of God in us, is indicative of his word as being

---

[72] See Barth, *Knowledge and Service of God*, 143.
[73] Torrance, *Atonement*, 431.

a word *to* us.[74] They are gift for they are words of eternal life, and they are a gift that claims. As those claimed, we do not look in frustration for what claimed existence looks like, however. We look to him, for in his personhood our faulty exercise of power – to use what we have been given to not believe – is forgiven. We are, as forgiven people, set upon a new path wherein the One who forgives also claims and converts to faith; he is the fulfillment of that which he claims: belief. He converts our false use of power, namely the 'power' to resist believing, in order to render it more in accord with his true exercise of power: the power to believe.

When Christian ethics is not afraid to speak of Jesus, to describe him in his person as the law of our being, and how he interposes himself between the law that he is and his followers, we better realize the extent to which all that we do has not only its beginning, but also its middle and its end in him. Jesus is not then another law – a 'Do this' that comes without the power to 'Do this'. He is not merely ethics' starting point; it is upheld by him as well. He makes it possible to do what he says to do because he has, in being raised from the dead, declared the poverty and powerlessness of all that would impede his community from precisely doing so. As such, he not only is the grounds for a truly new exercise of power but is also at the same time the one who concurrently enacts that new exercise, freely calling men and women to become participant in that enactment by the power of the Spirit.

It is my contention that such an emphasis is the only way in which ethics can rightly honor the Creator/creature distinction. If we are indeed creatures, we cannot extend or realize what is properly the Creator's work: eternal life. In the instance of John 5, what is properly the Creator's work is the negation of all that would prevent creation itself from conforming to his altogether good purposes for it. This is to say that the creature cannot defeat unbelief and its firstfruits sin and death; only the Creator may. Sin and death have no future. The creature has been liberated to be a creature, which means not to extend or realize the Creator's work anew, but simply to live transparently to it. It is to live as if the Creator's work is *present* to the creature and yet at the same time withdrawn 'from contemporaneous contact within history for reasons of mercy'.[75] And because we are not dealing with some vague presence but with

---

[74] See John 5.42.
[75] Torrance, *Atonement*, 431.

a very particular and personalizing presence, an unsubstitutable identity and therefore a definite identity that transforms or makes righteous, our humanity is thereby restored and renewed.[76] To be human is not to try to do what is properly the work of the Creator's power – vanquish unbelief. Rather, it is to become aligned with that power that is present and at work 'making all things (*poiō panta*) new', including this unnamed man (Rev. 21.5). In the ministry of Jesus, unbelief is not only *declared* to be judged. The declaration or announcement that it is judged – the central teaching of the ministry of Jesus – is a declaration that renders unbelieving men and women alive. It converts them: 'Anyone who hears (*akouōn*) my word...has eternal life' (John 5.24). For it calls them out of dehumanizing modes of being and remakes them in such a way that they are capable of really conforming to the victory achieved by the new Adam over the old.

THE MORAL SIGNIFICANCE OF THE PRESENCE OF CHRIST'S POWER: IN RELATIONSHIP TO THE THEODICY QUESTION

At this point in the argument, one could suggest that there is not enough material present here for pastoral or moral policy; that, in effect, the ontology – the metaphysical basis of ethics – I am proposing simply runs out of steam when it comes to engendering particulars, that it is indeed not concrete enough. Perhaps this is a way of responding to Hauerwas's worry about Barth's theology and ethics and of Bonhoeffer's too. Deeply sympathetic to Barth as he is, Hauerwas avers 'that Barth may have given an account of Christian doctrine in which the material conditions necessary to make doctrine intelligible were not accounted for sufficiently'.[77] Following Barth's cues, I have engaged in description of the way things are with a view to John 5: Jesus' ministry, his personhood and the command ingredient in it. This not only makes the constitutive difference for knowing how things are: he is working to make sure that things more nearly resemble the way they should be. Hauerwas would concur that this is the task of theology: 'Barth's recovery of the apocalyptic

---

[76] This is what I take to be the work of God in Christ as expressed by the Greek word *dikaiosunē* (righteousness). That is, 'God not only *declares* righteous but actually *makes* righteous.' Fleming Rutledge, *Not Ashamed of the Gospel: Sermons from Paul's Letter to the Romans* (Grand Rapids, MI: Eerdmans, 2007), 5.

[77] Stanley Hauerwas, *Hannah's Child: A Theological Memoir* (Grand Rapids, MI: Eerdmans, 2010), 87.

character of Christian convictions was a rational acknowledgement
that we cannot divorce our descriptions of the way the world is from
how we are to live and what we must be if we are to describe the world
rightly.'[78] Description of Christian convictions, in other words, is a
profoundly self-implicating undertaking. The description of Christ's
identity is also a description of the law; his personhood implicates.
This is Hauerwas's way – which is Barth's way – of resisting the charge
that description in the end is ultimately formalistic. That said, there is
a moment in Hauerwas's account regarding 'the material conditions
necessary to make doctrine intelligible', or, more specifically, 'the
necessity of the church's materiality as the precondition for being
able to articulate the difference God makes for knowing the way
things are' that is important to engage, as I turn briefly to the matter
of the moral significance of the presence of Christ's power.

I want to sound a different note from Hauerwas, namely that the
doctrine of Christ's person in its eternal, contemporary and advent
character does not require preconditions as far as its intelligibility is
conceived. Part of the point in offering a reading of John 5 is to show
that healings as ingredient in Jesus' ministry are radically *gratuitous*.
To be sure, Jesus calls forth belief; that is the creature's chief work,
even as belief is capacitated in us by him through the Spirit. But
there are no material conditions in place for an unnamed man to
be recipient of his healing work. I worry, then, about the notion of
the church's materiality, not because the Christian confession Jesus is
Lord does not take up space and effectively gather a community, but
rather because the language of pre-condition may detract from the
sheer grace of Christ who in an unconditioned sense wills to establish
his rule where there is absolutely nothing correspondent to it.

And so, when it comes to the question of the 'pre-conditions' for
being able to articulate the difference that the ministry, passion, death,
resurrection, ascension, session and coming again of he who fulfills
the covenant makes, I hesitate to say there are such. If we believe
that Jesus Christ is the great humanizing presence of God, as we
must, the perennial questions raised under the umbrella of theodicy
certainly point to how Christian confession very often originates *ex
nihilo*. If anything, the matter of natural evil – think the tsunami of
26 December 2004 – removes any temptation to suggest that the new
creation present as the firstfruits of Christ's resurrection from the
dead is present in unveiled fashion. Indeed, to sketch what kinds of

[78] Hauerwas, *Hannah's Child*, 264.

moral policy particulars might be appropriate to the belief that the power present and at work now in the ministry of Jesus is also cosmic power, proleptically revealed in the healing of the sick man, reminds us that God is really the 'pre-condition' for being able to articulate God. Now that is not to deny that God uses human witnesses to attest his Word and Spirit; but it is to say that Christ's power is present more of the time in a manner that is utterly uncatchable: creating witnesses, people of faith where there are none.

Jesus Christ is the *kosmokrator* (ruler of the universe). In John's language, he is the judge who delivers not only men and women from the powers of sickness, but also the cosmos which is in some measure subject, contrary to its will, to those very same powers. Indeed, the created world, which is to be a theater of God's glory, can be but so often is precisely the opposite. Again, one need only recall the devastating tsunami. One might and should ask: Why? Surely God can handle our lament. But more importantly, perhaps one should ask what kinds of actions might be appropriate to a people who believe that such wanton destruction of human life by the sea is *not* how things are supposed to be. That people began in the midst of horrendous grief to rebuild homes is indicative, I believe, of a not so subtle conviction that such ferocious displays of the power of nature are *not* in line with how things are supposed to be. The God of the Gospel is not naked causality; one cannot draw a straight line between 'natural evil' and 'God's will'. That people began to rebuild in earnest is testimony, I think, to an instinct that attests that there is more: wanton destruction of life is not in keeping with the grain of the universe.

Perhaps what is most problematic in the notion of either pre- or post- conditions for the intelligibility of Christian doctrine is the lack of an eschatological moment. I say lack because doctrine – description of how things are – is indicative of a new world, a new creation that is present as an imperative. Theodicies are all about giving an account of material conditions in accord with what was and is passing away – the world of the first Adam. Acts of faith, hope and love in response to what should not have been are thus appropriate to the way things are and will more so be. But we cannot specify in advance what the particulars of those acts might be. Jesus Christ as *kosmokrator* and humanizer of the cosmos is not another way of talking about causal forces. One cannot equate events of natural evil with his governance or rule of the world. That such things happen and will continue to happen is *not* evidence of his power. On the contrary, it is evidence of the quasi-independent powers of sin and death, which cause the creation 'to groan in labour pains', and subject it to a bondage not of its own making (Rom. 8.27). God's power – the power that raises Jesus from the dead and is breathed upon us by the Spirit – is not what causes everything to happen. To be sure, the Father in the Son by the Spirit is doing something. However, things that contradict their doing do happen, and they ought not to be explained away. That said, the human is not left inert in the face of them. Rather than trying to explain *why* events such as this happen, events which are indicative of a cosmos profoundly off kilter, the Christian is to point to the power that humanizes and thus to become participant in it.

The power resplendent in the ministry of Jesus humanizes in the sense that it mortifies our desire to answer why – it lets the screams be – even as it re-contextualizes those screams. That is, the world that suffers such cataclysmic events is a world held fast by the promise of personal, societal and cosmic restoration, the firstfruits of which is Jesus' resurrection from the dead and his breathing of the Spirit. When men and women engage in acts of service and compassion in obedience and faith on the part of those who have suffered the events of a cosmos in subjection to the powers, their acts are 'a sign of the ultimate Word of restoration, healing, and perfection of all things'.[79] Indeed, disorder on such a horrendous scale is to be contextualized 'for the sake of ultimate reconciliation to the true order of being'.[80] Such an understanding is relevant to the articulation of pastoral and moral policy directives, inasmuch as it points to a kind of eschatological reserve. Restoration will be manifest unto all precisely because there has been restoration. The past is our best guide to the present and future. And as such, the past disciplines our attempt to dull the screams; we learn to let them be precisely because we know them to be enveloped by the presence of a particular and definite mercy. Instead of asking 'why', we are to *do* something: indeed, we are to take up the mat and walk and to help those who cannot do the same.

The power at work in Jesus' ministry is unitive. The Spirit's power by which Father and Son are united anew in the resurrection and their fellowship and communion restored, is power that discloses being's true order. The natural world *is* to be a theater of life; yet it is no longer able to be such as a consequence of the fall, and our

[79] Ray S. Anderson, *On Being Human: Essays in Theological Anthropology* (Pasadena, CA: Fuller Seminary Press, 1982), 129.
[80] Anderson, *Being Human*, 129.

willing acquiescence in the fall of our first-parents. Its disorderly character points to the more fundamental disorder of a humanity estranged from its Creator. The business of the Gospel is to *contextualize* the disorder prevalent in the cosmos. The enmity on the part of humanity to God which funds disorder on a cosmic scale is circumscribed by the power of the Gospel, the power that compels the human to witness in word and deed to a power that 'executes judgment' and will accordingly reward those who have done good, 'to the resurrection of life' (John 10.29). What are we to do in the face of natural evil? Good, and be ready to be surprised at the forms it may take.

When one reads the last two chapters of the Book of Revelation, one gets a sense of this. Revelation is a book that never separates the doctrine of creation from that of reconciliation and redemption. 'Creation is not "back there", though there is a "back there" character to creation. Rather, creation names God's continuing action, God's unrelenting desire for us to want to be loved by that life manifest in Christ's life, death, and resurrection.'[81] Put differently, 'It is God the Creator of all reality who, in faithfulness to his creation, acts in Christ to reclaim and renew his whole creation.'[82] The power at work proleptically in the ministry of Jesus and fully disclosed in his resurrection is indeed a power that reclaims and renews the whole creation, delivering it from the threat of nothingness – which is disorder – and rendering it transparent to his restorative presence. Thus the kind of pastoral policy that follows from the contemporaneity of Jesus' person, and thus ministry, is a policy that eschews the answering of the why questions on their own terms. It does so in favor of pointing to the Creator's purpose for all of creation as one of being transparent to the power, truth and love present in the life, passion, death, resurrection and ascension of Jesus Christ. The whole of the cosmos, of creation, lies in its being made *for* Another who wills life for it. This One has said Yes to the cosmos in the most unequivocal way imaginable in his ministry to his people vindicated by his resurrection from the dead. He says yes to life and thus encourages *revolt* in the face of death. Death is not the last word. Rebuilding in the face of utter devastation suggests such; so, too, in the case of care for

---

[81] Hauerwas, *Hannah's Child*, 158.
[82] Richard Bauckham, *The Theology of the Book of Revelation* (Cambridge: Cambridge University Press, 1993), 163.

the sick and the lame, which anticipates the day when Christ's advent presence, his eschatological presence, will be all in all.

CONCLUSION

I claim that an account of reality matters for ethics. What Webster writes in relationship to the nature, location and reception of Scripture can be said of ethics: metaphysics governs ethics.[83] Reality is the communicative presence of an eternal and therefore contemporary person. The claim made about reality is coterminous with his person. That is, if you will, the 'theology proper' portion of the essay and of the chapter. But this is a work in ethics, too, and 'ethics is a name for expressing the practical character of theological speech'.[84] The practical character is dependent, I have argued, upon the proper character. This essay is not an attempt simply to see the world differently. It is an attempt to unfold conceptually what is really drastically simple: 'the very work I [Jesus] am doing (*apestalken*)' (John 5.36).[85]

And so, we do *see* the universe differently and seek to act in accord with and to correspond to its grain. The grain is there, to be sure; but the grain *is* operative and expansive and is, as such, *determining*. And here lies the heart of the intervention for which this essay is necessary. The ministry of Jesus determines and is intrinsic to the recovery of the basic grammar that should constitute our lives as Christians. His personhood as personhood which implicates is reality, that which constitutes our world and indeed our lives is present in such a way that our descriptions of the way things are must be subject to a 'going on'. The person and work of the mediator – in the case of this chapter, his ministry – matters for our description of reality. Without recourse to him, reality's dynamic character is eclipsed, and also the sense that reality is a going on, a happening, the presence of the apocalypse awaiting its final unveiling. 'Very truly, I tell you, the hour is coming, and is now here, when the dead will hear (*akousousin*) the voice of the Son of God, and those who hear (*akousantes*) will live' (John 5.25).

In sum, it is my judgment that the power at work in the ministry of Jesus is power that heals humanity. To be fully human is to be an active

---

[83] 'Metaphysics governs reception.' See John Webster, 'Resurrection and Scripture', in *Christology and Scripture: Interdisciplinary Perspectives*, ed. Andrew T. Lincoln and Angus Paddison (London: T&T Clark, 2008), 150.

[84] Hauerwas, *Hannah's Child*, 237.

[85] This is from *apostellō*, meaning to send.

participant in his life-giving power and presence. This is power which says No to unbelief, thereby destroying it. And it is a power present and contemporary to us in the Spirit. Indeed, it is breathed upon us by him through his Spirit. It orders us toward what *is*, to be shaped by what is going on. What *is* going on is precisely that a new world has been brought and is being brought into being. That world is a world in which a new kind of power is at work: the power to believe. We as God's people believe, albeit provisionally, because to believe is to do good and thus to be transparent to the God whose exercise of power is not vindictive but restorative. It restores inasmuch as it converts and generates hearers. Faith pardons false exercises of our agency – 'It is now lawful for you to carry your mat' – and in so doing claims us for the true exercise of our agency, the firstfruits being belief (John 5.10). That exercise, on the level of moral policy, eschews answering the theodicy question on its own terms. It does so in favour of witness to the true order of things: *creatio ex nihilo*. The Gospel thus contextualizes the disorder represented by natural evil; for the Gospel, as true order, the order that *is* becoming, forbids us from equating the order resplendent in Jesus' ministry with causality. It is Jesus' power which throws the furniture of such an understanding around, calling us, as Jesus did with the ill man in John 5, to witness to the ultimate and true Word of power about which Moses wrote, one which heals and claims us, so that we might live transparently to how things *shall* be: 'so that you will be astonished' (John 5.20).

Chapter 3

ON THE PRESENCE OF CHRIST'S TRUTH

As with the other main chapters, this chapter sketches an account of ethics that takes seriously Jesus' ongoing presence and ministry as 'the author and perfecter of our faith' (Heb. 12.2). It offers an account of ethics from the side of God and thus from the side of the human being. Jesus Christ is the One who authors and perfects not only the right exercise of power but, in the case of this chapter, truth: he wills that the truth he is be realized in us. Accordingly, truth cannot be either a body of facts or a storehouse of propositions about the way things purportedly are. Truth is indeed identical to a very particular person, Jesus the Christ, and to his ministry, cross, resurrection, ascension and session. Ethics is simply a matter of acts that are caught up in the truth that he is, the transfiguring truth that is his rule. 'Created being is being in this divine act of transformation.'[1] Accordingly, ethics is bound up with the movement of One ahead of itself, and its task, as this chapter unfolds it, is to become transparent to it.

The trustworthy and sufficient witness to the truth is Holy Scripture. Scripture is the appointed location from where the truth speaks so as to form us into his witnesses. So John 18.37: 'Everyone who belongs to the truth (*alētheias*) listens (*akouei*) to my voice.' The first section of this chapter is just that: a fresh hearing, I trust, of the voice of truth as narratively rendered. By listening to Jesus' self-witness in the trial scenes of John's Gospel, a foundation is laid for the pursuit of the chapter's second task: a descriptive account of the eternal *identity* of the truth as the basis for his contemporaneity. The narrative depicts an agent who, although cast out for a time, is, by virtue of his resurrection, said to be *present* and at work here and now in his Spirit

---

[1] Webster, 'Resurrection and Scripture', in *Christology and Scripture*, 141.

in a way that is rooted in and underwritten by his eternality. His 'continuing ministry' is the reiteration in a new key of his immanent life.[2] After engaging in descriptive work regarding the eternal identity and therefore presence of Christ as the truth, I inquire in the third section after the matter of law or command, specifically what kind of law or command does his self-presentation as the truth in the trial scenes generate? I do so because an account of his immanent life is not only the guarantor of his contemporaneity but also one that has considerable moral force. There is an imperative, a 'Do this' which arises from an account of his person in the form of a command to truthfulness. In the conclusion of this chapter I reflect, briefly, on the moral significance and the pastoral resources engendered by the exegesis as well as the description of the indicative and imperative character of Christ's presence.

JOHN'S WITNESS TO TRUTH: JOHN 18.1–19.42

This section describes Jesus as one who, on the basis of the trial scenes in John's Gospel, presents himself as the truth. We can see this beginning to take shape in his self-identification upon his arrest, which issues with the explosive announcement: 'I am he (*egō eimi*)' (John 18.5). Explosive because Jesus' declaration to the soldiers, chief priests, and the Pharisees who come to arrest him is not without effect. Indeed, his self-declaration is said by John to cause them to step back and fall 'to the ground' (John 18.6). That they fall to the ground is no surprise; for the 'I am he' *is* divine revelation. It is the announcement of his rule even over the power that will, for a time, defeat him. 'Revelation is rule', the very revelation of the rule of truth.[3] Truth unmasks falsehood. In particular, truth unmasks the assumptions of those who in the narrative assume that their agency is ultimate. One of the great ironies of the betrayal and arrest of Jesus is that those who come to arrest Jesus actually think that they know what he is all about; they mistakenly assume that they know the identity of the One for whom they are looking. The chief priests, together with the Pharisees, expect to find one who is guilty of blasphemy; and as far as the Romans are concerned, they expect to find one guilty of sedition.

---

[2] The language of 'continuing ministry' is taken from Walker, Introduction to Torrance, *Atonement*, liii.

[3] Webster, 'Resurrection and Scripture', in *Christology and Scripture*, 152.

But the One whom they actually find upsets such easy, unfounded and closed assumptions about himself.

The utterance 'I am he' is the majestic utterance of a King. As a majestic utterance, it is *effective*: again, they fell 'to the ground'. Hoskyns comments, 'To the author of the Fourth Gospel the words of Jesus are not primarily teaching about God and Truth and immortality, but rather, *effective* [emphasis mine], creative, life-giving utterances, which effect the transformation from death to life and from dead to living flesh.'[4] Jesus does not teach the truth. He declares himself to be the truth, the truth who reconciles by subjecting himself to those who falsely assume that their agency is supreme and unassailable. Jesus' self-description in terms of 'I am he' is thus a not-so-subtle reminder that his self-presentation – his presence – is never without effect. Indeed, it gives life and it can condemn. Thus, even those who do not respond to his Kingship in faith are nonetheless profoundly affected by it. As the narrative unfolds we see the extent to which the person he is does not engender indifference: one either shouts 'Crucify him!' or else one gathers with the disciple whom Jesus loved and his mother and attends to him at the foot of his cross.[5]

Barth is especially helpful for unfolding the contours of the programmatic announcement 'I am he'. Barth describes the biblical witness to Jesus Christ as a witness in which Jesus is the acting subject. Barth writes, 'He [Jesus] is the Subject of His history as attested in Scripture'.[6] Jesus' history, as narrated for us in John's Gospel, is a history that is disclosive of his identity. And so, to know this One, this subject, is to attend to his history, to what he actually says and does. The declaration of his identity in this scene as the 'I am he' – reminiscent of course of Exodus 3.14 – marks the beginning of the passion narrative wherein the Jewish and Gentile world evidence their unbelief in relation to the Lord's self-declaration. But even as Jesus is pushed further and further toward death, the narrative announces in no uncertain terms that this is a history in which Jesus *is* Lord, in which he remains acting subject.

Contrary to what might seem to be the case, Christ is utterly sovereign even as he submits himself to the sphere of sovereignty whose defining mark is unbelief and falsehood. 'So if you are looking for me, let these men go', says Jesus (John 18.8). In Jesus' response

---

[4] Hoskyns, *Fourth Gospel*, 1:340.
[5] See John 19.25-27.
[6] *CD* IV/3, 39.

there is complete and utter self-control on his part when confronted with the claim of another exercise of agency, another sovereignty which would have us believe in its ultimacy, its truthfulness. The 'I am', even as he will soon be swallowed up by death, is sovereign even over the eventual roar of the opposition – 'Crucify him!' – that will soon swallow him up.[7]

After Jesus is arrested, he is brought before the high priest and thereafter Pilate. Interspersed between Jesus' interrogations, in which he is not only questioned but questions, one finds two denials by Peter. Twice Peter says 'I am not (*Ouk eimi*) one of this man's disciples' (John 18.17, 25). Peter's response to the unsettling events that surround him is to deny what he is: a disciple. Whereas Jesus' response to his interlocutors throughout the narrative is always congruent with his identity: 'I am he'. His self-attestation, the agreement of what he does (reveal his reconciliation) with who he is (reconciliation), is perfect and true. I am the one who will 'drink the cup that the Father has given to me' (John 18.11). For me not to drink the cup would be for me to evade my identity as the truth who effects and proclaims truth by suffering falsehood and thereby negating it.

John 18.28–19.16a is the culmination of Jesus' passion. Therein is narrated Jesus' trial before Pilate. What is crucial to note is that this is a trial about truth, indeed truth's basic character, and truth's power. Can such truth, Jesus as *the* truth, found a Kingdom? So Pilate asks, incredulously, 'Are you the King of the Jews?' (John 18.33) Jesus answers, 'You say that I am a king (*Basileus*). For this I was born, and for this I came into the world, to testify (*martupēsō*) to the truth (*alētheia*). Everyone who belongs to the truth listens (*akouei*) to my voice' (John 18.37). The passion narrative of Jesus is where, even though he is effectively being shoved out of the world, his voice is the strongest. He has a voice, and his voice is the voice of truth. The voice of his rule is aligned with the order of being; the very truth he is, he instantiates.

We rightly read the trial scenes in John as denoting a remarkable contrast between Pilate and Jesus, between Pilate and the Jews (and Jesus, too), and Jesus and Judas. In different ways, Pilate and the Jews as well as Judas function as agents for God's purposes in accomplishing the world's salvation. But their agency is purely negative. It

---

[7] The language of 'swallowing up' is drawn from Isa. 25.6-9, wherein the Lord God, the host of the great eschatological banquet, 'will swallow up death forever'.

is the darkness which supposes that it can overcome the light. The darkness, however, is circumscribed, just like that of the soldiers, chief priests and Pharisees who come to arrest Jesus. The voice of King Jesus goes forth, and those who belong 'to the truth' listen to him.

There is, Pilate avers, 'no case against him' (John 18.38). That there is no case against him should hardly surprise us. Calvin comments, 'For it is impossible that He to whom the office of maintaining the truth has been divinely given and in whom its care is innate by nature should teach what is untrue.'[8] He cannot contradict himself, and those on the side of truth, as Pilate is but only for a moment, acknowledge that there is not any falsehood in what he says, for what he says is disclosive of who he is. Pilate's announcement to the Jews – 'I find no case against him' – is really his own answer to the question which he posed earlier to Jesus: 'Are you the King of the Jews?' (John 18.38, 33).

Falsehood and untruth, however, are not interested in listening; they have already made up their mind. There is not any room for disruption: they are by nature closed. To put matters more technically, there is in the case of Jesus' interlocutors the profound lack of an eschatological moment. Indeed, what is so shocking in the trial scenes in John's passion narrative is the rigidity of his opponents' denunciation, in particular Pilate's seeming mockery of the whole question of truth. Pilate's famous question 'What is truth?' reeks of cynicism (John 18.38). Insofar as Pilate and the Jewish leadership are concerned, there cannot be any answer to the question. Truth 'lies far higher than the grasp of the human mind'.[9] Truth is not a possession to be held, but a person who is himself one who confronts. Truth, then, is not a distinct and remote reality. Truth is present in the form of a person who is a King, whose Kingship is truth, and whose Kingship suffers at the hands of falsehood.

It is the height of irony that Pilate's second intervention with Jesus is one in which the Jewish leadership invokes the law as the basis for their denunciations of Jesus.[10] They cannot listen to and cannot hear Jesus, precisely because they claim to 'have a law, and according

  [8] John Calvin, *Calvin's New Testament Commentaries*, Part 2, *The Gospel According to St. John* (Grand Rapids, MI: Eerdmans, 1959), 167.

  [9] Calvin, *Gospel According to St. John*, 168.

  [10] See John 19.8-11. For the Jewish leadership, the Bible is understood as 'law'. Moody Smith, *Gospel of John*, 50.

to the law he ought to die because he has claimed to be the Son of God' (John 19.7). That which anticipates him, that which he fulfills, that through which his Father spoke so as to form a people into his people, now becomes the grounds of judgment for his Son who is the law's *telos* and its very fulfillment.[11] There is Moses's law, no doubt; but there is also a human being before them, who testifies to the truth and who claims to *be* the truth, the incarnation of the Word.[12] However, the 'law' will soon supersede the person, for the law of God whose sum is the command to love God and the neighbor as oneself cannot be heard.[13] It is mute. Jesus is handed over. The truth – the 'I am he' – becomes subject to crass manipulation (John 18.6). Rather than ruling, he is ruled over. 'Thus Christ is *the* rejected of God, for God makes Himself rejected in Him, and has Himself alone tasted to the depths all that rejection means and necessarily involves.'[14]

One of the chief questions that Jesus' trial scene poses is this: Does Jesus' passion's culmination in the trial scenes speak today, do these scenes live? Do they function as entities confined to the past, or do they do 'their work in an immanently conceived communication field'?[15] I ask because it would be all too easy to read the passion and thus the trial scenes in John as a narrative which presents the claims of a Jew whom Pilate calls both 'the man' and 'your King' as identity descriptions of a *past* agent (John 19.5, 14). But what if 'the man' and 'your King' is still *the* man and King? Without taking away from the historical particularity of the narrative, our task in this chapter is to hear the narrative as a narrative which bespeaks the identity of One who as *this* One – the subject of this history – *is* present and as such ministering the truth.

Although the focus of the narrative is one in which the truth is handed over and exorcised, the truth is actually – rather arrestingly – magnified in its willingness to be cast out. John is at pains to attest Jesus as the King of truth who 'manifests His royal power not by force, but by the witness He bears to the Truth'.[16] His power is his witness to the truth that He is. And it is effective – but not effective in the way we would generally assume. In a world that cannot hear the One before it, Christians must be content to live in the light of a

---

[11] See Rom. 10.4.

[12] See John 10.14.

[13] Mt. 22.37-40.

[14] *CD* II/2, 496, original emphasis.

[15] Webster, 'Resurrection and Scripture', in *Christology and Scripture*, 145.

[16] Hoskyns, *Fourth Gospel*, 2:619.

King whose voice *finishes* not only the world's deafness and blindness but also their own, by suffering the wrath of its untruth. Indeed, Jesus puts an end to both his own people's and the Gentiles' deafness and blindness by suffering it. He overturns his own people's verdict and the Roman officials, too, partaking of their verdict through acceptance of it. Indeed, Jesus reigns in the passion narrative in John. His being handed over is demonstration of the truth and power he is. He reigns to the extent that he can suffer the most humiliating of verdicts and, as we will see, overcome it.

'Here is your King!' Pilate announces toward the end of the sixth scene (John 19.14). What he says is true, but not exhaustively so. For he is not only the King of the Jews, but of the Gentiles as well. This is what Pilate does not understand. 'There is only one authority and therefore one Kingdom.'[17] The truth that Jesus is, acts as the great relativizer in the passion narrative. To Pilate Jesus says, 'You would have no power (*exousian*) over me unless it had been given you from above' (John 19.11). The power that Pilate exercises is circumscribed by a power 'from above' that is more powerful than that of the emperor. The truth of Jesus' Kingship lies in its ability, then, to re-contextualize all claims to the contrary, such that temporal and spatial existence be existence in his presence.[18] Jesus is, according to the leadership of his own people, guilty of sedition. 'Everyone who claims to be a king sets himself against the emperor' (John 19.12). And because Pilate accepts their claim – 'We have no king but the emperor' – he too is guilty of sedition (John 19.15). Both have denied God's sovereignty, and in the case of the Jews have 'abdicated the right to be His chosen people'.[19] The voice of the people triumphs, the voice by which they forfeit – but only for a time – who and whose they are. In D. Moody Smith's words, Jesus' people function as 'symbols of [the] human rejection of God's revelation in Jesus. So they become representatives of the world in a negative sense,'[20] It is their rejection, however, which Jesus bears not only for their sake but for the sake of the life of the world.

It is in the trial scenes that we see the profound confusion of the ultimate and the penultimate. To be sure, this is Bonhoeffer's language, language he uses to describe the character of the God/

[17] Ward, *Politics of Discipleship*, 293.
[18] See further Webster, 'Resurrection and Scripture', in *Christology and Scripture*, 147.
[19] Hoskyns, *Fourth Gospel*, 2:631.
[20] Moody Smith, *Gospel of John*, 56.

world relationship.[21] And it is language which may serve to illuminate and further describe what is taking place in the trial scenes. What Pilate and the Jews – Jesus' own people – are guilty of, is the confusion of the ultimate with the penultimate. There is Jesus' Kingship and the emperor's kingship. These kingships, so the chief priests would have us believe, are mutually exclusive. The chief priests say, 'We have no king but the emperor' (John 19.15). But Jesus is a King who claims all spheres or realms of creaturely life for himself. Indeed, his Kingship – what is ultimate – judges the penultimate, and thereby establishes the right relationship between it and himself as the location of his recon-ciling self-communication. Indeed, life (including government) is true to its God-given 'mandate', inasmuch as it in a manner appro-priate to itself, prepares, according to Bonhoeffer, the way for the coming of Christ.[22] Although Bonhoeffer is thinking primarily within a Pauline idiom in the following statement, it can nonetheless serve to illuminate what is happening in John's narrative. 'Since God's justification by grace and by faith alone remains in every respect the ultimate word, now we must also speak of penultimate things not as if they had some value of their own, but so as to make clear their relation to the ultimate.'[23] What Pilate and the chief priests suspect is that there is not any relationship between Jesus' words – 'You would have no power over me unless it had been given you from above' – and the ultimate, the ultimate being what they *think* they know to be true about themselves and what they do (John 19.11). For the Jews, there is 'the law'. And that is all there is: the law without a lawgiver and *telos*. Jesus' people mistakenly assume that the law has a value of its own, rather than being something like a tutor, which enables God's people to live truly in this world as his covenant people.

What happens is that the powerful among Jesus' people and among the Roman powers find it too hard to hear Jesus' words. So he is crucified. Christ comes to this world to be its King. He is born a King. 'No one can hinder Christ's coming, but we can oppose that coming in grace.'[24] And oppose we do: 'There they crucified him' (John 19.19). But even as he is crucified, he announces from the Cross that 'It is finished (*Tetelestai*)' (John 19.30). Indeed, the passion

---

[21] See *DBW*, vol. 6, *Ethics*, 146–70.

[22] There are four divine mandates for Bonhoeffer: marriage and family, work (what is elsewhere called 'culture'), government and church. See further *DBW*, vol. 6, *Ethics*, 388–89 n. 2.

[23] *DBW*, vol. 6, *Ethics*, 151.

[24] *DBW*, vol. 6, *Ethics*, 162.

and the crucifixion finishes falsehood's claims. The cross finishes the sordid history of Jewish and Gentile humanity's attempts to supersede the ultimate, to listen to its own voice, establish its own kings, and claim for itself to be the measure and arbiter of truth.

The trilingual title (Hebrew, Latin and Greek) 'Jesus of Nazareth, the King of the Jews', indicates that the death of truth's voice brings a new family into being: a family of hearers and witnesses to what is heard (John 19.19). 'The Church proceeds from the sacrifice of the Son of God.'[25] What differentiates the Christian community from all other communities, albeit often only provisionally, is that it believes in solidarity with all people that 'it is finished' (John 19.30). That is, it confesses as one of the basic acts of its life, that the victim whose voice was extinguished in fact does finish – indeed, destroys – all that would cause his voice not to be heard, his Kingship ignored. His obedience unto death accomplishes his people's salvation and the world's, thereby demonstrating him to be one who rules always as a reconciling and revealing presence.

This perhaps points to the significance of 'blood' and 'water' pouring forth from the crucified One's side (John 19.34). Jesus is the Savior of the world; Jews and Gentiles are cleansed, reconciled and enlivened by his blood. His rule, the very enactment of the truth he is, reconciles in such a way as to bring forth a new community. ' "Woman, here is your son". Then he said to the disciple, "here is your mother" ' (John 19.26, 27). We become brothers and sisters to one another before the crucified. In a sense, we are to take one another into our homes, to exercise hospitality to one another, as an act that corresponds to the new humanity that is brought into being, the second Adam's very re-capitulation and re-contextualization of the corrupt history of the first Adam.

In sum, in this section I have sought to describe the theological significance of Jesus' passion, the trial scenes in John, with a view to describing Jesus' sacrifice on the cross as the culmination of his enactment of the truth and the definitive act of his Kingship. Jesus suffers lies, accusations of sedition, the blasphemy of his own people, and the blessing of the Gentile rulers with respect to their approval of his own people's blasphemy. Our challenge is thus to hear in all of this an explosive description of the identity of an Agent whose agency is extinguished but only for a time, and thus as an agent who is, as resurrected and ascended, our contemporary. Indeed, our

---

[25] Hoskyns, *Fourth Gospel*, 2:631.

challenge is to hear the One whose history is narrated here as *with* us, as speaking to us, as interrogating us, and thus as putting us (and the world) on trial. In order to describe the contours of his continuing ministry via the trial scenes, his passion and death, we turn to Barth and his treatment of the prophetic office of Jesus Christ in §69 of *CD* IV/3. It is there that we find many resources for describing his personhood's eternality – its immanent character – as that which give rise to his contemporaneity.

A TRUTHFUL PRESENCE: ETERNAL AND CONTEMPORARY

In the previous section, I argued that there is a person who as the truth establishes his rule in the world by suffering and, in so doing, negating the unbelief of his people and the acquiescence of the Roman leadership in that unbelief. To attend to the identity of this One as narratively rendered is to do the hard work of Christology. To do the work of Christology is to re-tell this history as a history that lives wholly and entirely by virtue of its acting subject. Barth writes, 'Christology is a narration of His history, and specifically of the shining of His light, the real speaking of the covenant, the revelation of reconciliation, the action of the Prophet Jesus Christ.'[26] Five directives regarding Christology's purpose and task are contained in Barth's statement. These directives shall establish a framework for this section, as I seek to describe Christ's personhood as the truth of God manifest in all its eternality and thus its contemporaneity as presented in the trial scenes of John's Gospel.

First, in an essay concerning ethics in the presence of Christ, it behooves us to consider his history. His history is the content of Christology, the very account of his person. Christology works with what is given: a definite and specific history. Accordingly, it is not so much a constructive undertaking as a descriptive one: it is a matter of telling his story. That is what we have done in part in the previous section. To do so is to gloss the passion (trial scenes) of Jesus with a view to the picture they provide of his identity. Jesus' identity is enacted in those scenes. Indeed, act and being are one in his person: he acts in accord with who he is, the truth he is. He always enacts who he is, true God and true man.

Second, Christology as a narration of Jesus' history is also the telling of the truth which shines in the midst of falsehood, suffering

---

[26] *CD* IV/3, 166.

lies even as it unmasks and finishes them. The trial scene demonstrates that the truth that Jesus is indeed unmasks the pretences of his Jewish and Gentile interlocutors. Moreover, I have intimated that the trial scenes are scenes which interrogate us as well. They function, one might say, in the present tense; they are light. The texts function in such a way because of their subject. Put more strongly, the history that is being told here is one that really shines. Accordingly, it is not the 'sign of a past communicative event'.[27] His history possesses a liveliness and vitality of its own which shines in the darkness of his world and ours too.

Pilate and his own people's response is a mirror of the world's response to Jesus' history. It would be all too easy to state that the truth that Jesus is, the truth that is proper to his person, has shone. Easy because we conceive of this history as temporally circumscribed because there is something more real – the here and now – into which an account of his person and thus his presence and ministry must fit. Quite the opposite: the light that he is shines, the truth that he is speaks, he reigns as King for 'time and space are "under his feet"' (Eph. 1.22).[28] To be sure, the operative force of the 'is', that Jesus *is* the truth, is certainly due to his resurrection. However, because he is raised, we must read the whole of history as a history that shines, as a history that appears to us on the basis of its own sovereign accord. It is a history disclosive of an identity that does not need us to make it shine but nonetheless incorporates us into its shining. Indeed, his history shines as a consequence and as an unfolding of the fact that he is 'the King of glory: resplendent, outgoing, and therefore eloquent'.[29]

Third, I have been mindful of the fact that the history of Jesus' passion is the culmination of his Father's covenantal dealings with his people. The history of Israel is a covenant history that speaks. Indeed, the history of Israel and its fulfillment in Christ speaks precisely because the One who is pushed out due to Israel's final 'No' is as it were raised from the dead. 'I have seen the Lord', announces Mary (John 20.18). And so, the history of the covenant is history *in* the present tense. This is neither to take away from the unsubstitutability of God's history with Israel nor from the promises and events constitutive of it. But it is to say that Israel's history is a representative

---

[27] Webster, 'Resurrection and Scripture', in *Christology and Scripture*, 147.
[28] Webster, 'Resurrection and Scripture', in *Christology and Scripture*, 140.
[29] Webster, 'Resurrection and Scripture', in *Christology and Scripture*, 141.

history with respect to the history of humankind; Israel's infidelity is a window to Gentile infidelity: 'All have sinned.'[30] The history of the covenant really does speak, then, for God's covenantal dealings with his chosen people are the rubric through which he addresses all people, speaks to all people and is present to all people. To tell the story of Jesus is to tell the history of a particular people, a history which possesses a remarkable concreteness and expansiveness inclusive as it is of the Gentiles: you and I. 'He is the one who has really bound himself in the freedom of his existence to me.'[31]

Fourth, that Jesus suffers falsehood and death as the truth means that he *reveals* what his passion and death accomplish – the finishing of falsehood and death, in short reconciliation. 'The revelation of reconciliation' is Barth's way of reminding us that what is accomplished in and by the life and death of Christ – namely, reconciliation, to use a Pauline idiom – is not ours (or the church's) to reveal, but rather is Christ's to reveal. The identity of Christ is as revealer. He is the revealer of the reconciliation that he is, and so calls us to acknowledge him as revealer. He reveals the truth that he is, the Kingdom of God which he proclaims, enacts, and identifies with himself. He is, one may also say, the revealer of the truthfulness that he is. He reveals and discloses the truth that he is. His truth is reconciliation, for by its demonstration he makes humanity his covenant partner and wills to make the creature participant in eternal life.[32]

This leads to Barth's fifth point regarding Christology: the man, the King Jesus Christ, is also as such a prophet. He proclaims the truth that he *is*. His identity is as the prophet. Jesus' history is a prophetic history, and so it possesses a remarkable propensity for bespeaking itself; it is luminous. The trial scenes can and do function as a mirror of human history because their subject is self-manifesting. His existence as the man who was handed over by Judas and by the chief priests and crucified by Pontius Pilate has 'range and significance'.[33] It is our task in this second section of the chapter to attend to its range and significance, to ask after the range and significance of his passion and death as narrated by John, to treat his range and significance as a function of his immanent identity. Our task is to describe, in other words, the ways in which Jesus is the announcing subject of

[30] Rom. 3.23.
[31] Bonhoeffer, *Christ the Center*, 48.
[32] *CD* II/2, 492.
[33] *CD* IV/3, 174.

his history. This is to be mindful of the manner in which he preaches his passion and in which the trial scenes *live* as disclosive of his identity, and thus unmask our perennial opposition to his presence.

These five points of Barth's are of particular significance for mapping the relationship between the past and the present, the then and there and the here and now, as well as the eternal and contemporary identity of the truth. In order to understand this significance, let us assume that Jesus proclaims himself as one who is put on trial and is crucified as 'the King' and 'the man'; let us assume, moreover, that Jesus Christ never ceases to announce to the world what he announced to Pilate: 'Everyone who belongs to the truth listens (*akouei*) to my voice' (John 18.37). The conflict between Jesus and Pilate, between Jesus and his own people, is a conflict which *is* contemporary, precisely because he, as the one who is led to be crucified, speaks, because his history lives. But it lives because he is the enfleshed *eternal* Word of the Father.

He is a prophet who proclaims himself as our contemporary, meaning just as King Jesus entered over two thousand years ago into his people's history of enmity with respect to his Father and his covenantal purposes for them, he continually ministers as One who enters into our history of enmity now, and savingly so. Herein lies the importance of Barth's fifth point for ethics. An ethics appropriate to the moment of Jesus' history that reconciles, primarily but not only his trial scenes and cross, is an ethics that recognizes that the very possibility of ethics is not generated from within the conditions of history. Moral action, in other words, is not created out of conditions that exist. Moral acts are, rather, most fundamentally, responses to the 'action of the prophet' and not to conditions immanent within history itself.[34] The action of the prophet who is history's origin and goal evokes activity commensurate with the origin and goal that he is: namely, the truth. That he can and does do so is because he eternally is, together with the Father and Spirit, One who can be and is himself even in the midst of profound opposition, because he is the Son of the Father. By virtue of his eternally being begotten of the Father, no

[34] This is but to say that there is no place for historicism in ethics, for in historicism 'history is left without a subject'. All that history has is itself. Ethics thus becomes an undertaking in which there is only the raw material of history with which to work. The good does not exist. From whence would we know of the good, if there were such a thing? History is a process which fulfills itself. 'History will declare its own meaning.' Oliver O'Donovan, *Resurrection and Moral Order: An Outline for Evangelical Ethics* (Grand Rapids, MI: Eerdmans, 1986), 60, 64.

amount of opposition can thwart the enactment of his identity and his mission: 'Before Abraham was, I am (*egō eimi*)'.

To the prophet Jesus Christ 'it is given to see and understand the doing of the will of God on earth'. The prophet 'is also charged to declare, expound and explain, and thus to mediate, his understanding [of the doing of the will of God on earth], thus enabling others to *participation* [emphasis mine] in what takes place'.[35] In other words, Jesus Christ, as the Prophet, does the will of God; he does what he is: God's will for humanity. And his prophecy as the will of God on earth is effective because he enables others to participate in what takes place in and through him: reconciliation. He forms us in accord with his action that we might live as those who are reconciled to the truth that he is, that we might be taken captive by his person as the revealer of the truth he is and accomplishes. This is to say that to describe the identity of this one as far as his passion and death are concerned, is to be drawn into his sphere, the sphere of truth, a 'spiritually visible reality to be seen'.[36] The truth that he is, is therefore not inert. Thus, in a section devoted to the eternal and contemporary identity of Christ as the truth, it can be said that he does not will to have himself, to be the person and thus the truth that he is, to keep his doing of the will of God, apart from others. Ethics is a function of his will that the truth he is be incarnated into us; for he is present only as One who gathers, upholds, and sends truthful people forth.

The truth of the prophet Jesus *is* constitutive of reality. Ontology matters for ethics, but not once again in a ' "like it or lump it" ' sense.[37] He is acting among us as he did; he is present now as then, unmasking our falsehood with respect to the truth, for that is who he is. 'As the ruling Jesus Christ lives, so he reveals... Jesus Christ's being is antecedently luminous, of itself making itself perceptible.'[38] Or, 'Jesus limited by time is not Jesus.'[39] That is not to suggest that his history is substitutable, that it is not 'once and for all' (Heb. 9.12). But it is to say that the 'for all' – the doing of the One who is our representative, the second Adam, the great recapitulator of fallen humanity – is remarkably expansive, because it is rooted in his being which of itself is ontologically, together with Father and Spirit, self-

---

[35] *CD* IV/3, 180.
[36] Webster, 'Resurrection and Scripture', in *Christology and Scripture*, 154.
[37] See *DBW*, vol. 8, *Letters and Papers*, 373.
[38] Webster, 'Resurrection and Scripture', in *Christology and Scripture*, 144.
[39] Bonhoeffer, *Christ the Center*, 54.

sufficient. As the One he is, he contains a profound summons; his history that calls for participation. That his being can do so is because it 'is antecedently luminous'. Christ is our contemporary because he is antecedent to us. But he does not will to be without us. Reality is thus not simply a given state of affairs which falls unforeseen upon us. Rather, reality is declared, expounded, explained, and mediated by One who enables others to participate in it. His immanent identity as that which grounds his economic identity includes us, therefore, the inheritors of the apostolic tradition, for he does not will to have himself without the apostolate and us (and one hopes all flesh) in them.

Dietrich Bonhoeffer's polemic against the reduction of ethics to principles is particularly important to hear at this point, if we are to offer a robust theological description of the eternal and contemporary character of this person as the Truth. 'We have abandoned the abstract notion, largely dominant in ethical thought, of an isolated individual who has available an absolute criterion by which to choose continually and exclusively between a clearly recognized good and a clearly recognized evil.'[40] Truth, when defined as an absolute criterion, is thus something at our disposal, something at hand – truth as a principle. And this is precisely what crucifies the Lord. 'We have a law (*nomon*)' (John 19.7). The law of God is indeed God's truth, God's Word by which God speaks and forms his people into his covenant people. But the law is self-effacing and it does not contain the power to bring about what it demands. Only in the Spirit can it be kept. Accordingly, the law is not an end in itself: its origin is the Lord. Law's end is the Lord, who gives the law as an instrument whereby fellowship and communion with himself is engendered. The law and therewith truth when understood in a constructivist or immanentist sense become a weapon. Fidelity to the letter of the law kills; law becomes something over which we preside, that which we control.

Bonhoeffer reminds us that there are not any absolute criteria or absolute truths for ethics. There is only a person whose identity is truth, whose voice is truth. 'I have spoken openly to the world; I have always taught in synagogues and in the temple, where all the Jews come together. I have said nothing in secret' (John 18.20). But truth, when conceived of as either an ideal or a quality, becomes closed unto itself and is no longer truly the truth. It becomes instead a first principle not subject to discernment in the power of the Spirit.

---

[40] *DBW*, vol. 6, *Ethics*, 219.

Stated differently, it is reified: what John's trial scenes disclose is the unwillingness and inability of people to hear what is said. 'You would have no power over me unless it had been given from above' (John 19.11). To be sure, the actors in the narrative exercise power; but it is from below and so is not in accord with the truth.

Precisely because the truth lives and speaks, it *is* as such transformative. Truth as ingredient in his personhood does not need to be applied. It only needs to be heard. In listening we are made new. Listening to the truth, however, is not a passive activity. Listening to this truth is transformative, precisely because the One who is truth integrates us and his Spirit into his history. His history – which is our history too as radically recapitulated – is a history which negates our history of falsehood and as such our history which refuses to hear. That negation is 'the cup that the Father has given' him to drink (John 18.11). And drink it he does. His determination, which is the determination of his Father, is to be the King of his people, and in being their King the King of the whole world. His determination is that all submit to his reign, the sovereign revelation of his determination. 'His Word is gloriously directed above all norms and therefore to sinful man resisting His glory.'[41] To the chief priests who answer his claim to Kingship with a motto quite similar to that used by Jewish anti-Roman revolutionaries – 'We have no king but the emperor' – he announces, in suffering their answer, his supreme authority and power over them (John 19.15b). This is the grain of the universe. The truth of Jesus achieves its presence amid the lies of this world, among the leaders of his people in the very act of its being extinguished. Were the truth he is not eternal and immanent, it would not be. But he can never be One whom he is not: 'Jesus Christ is the same yesterday and today and forever' (Heb. 13.8).

Jesus dies as one faithful to his Father's purposes. His truth is cruciform in character, meaning it contains a startling negation and affirmation. Negation because the Jewish and Gentile world says No to the man whose 'Kingdom is not from this world' (John 18.36). The world's negation is, the world thinks, the last word. 'We have done away with the mischief maker, this blasphemer; we have honored God's law in doing so', the world boasts. But really, Gentiles, in collusion with the Jews and Judas, have capitulated to the most inhumane of forces. It is ironic that Pilate says to the chief priests and police, after finding no case against Jesus, 'Here is the man

---

[41] *CD*, IV/3, 195.

(*anthrōpos*)' (John 19.5). I say ironic because here *is* the man who has the power to put to rest the inhumanity that is about to swallow him up. Here is *the* man, the man who humanizes the world. That truth does so is because truth is a particular person; it is ingredient in him. And the way in which this person – the true man – finishes acts of inhumanity great and small, and thus humanizes, is by suffering them. This is the great Yes to humanity that he is. Our No to his voice, to the truth, is that which God uses to achieve our good. The No is indeed inclusive of the Yes of God to us.[42]

Barth writes, 'It [reconciliation] achieves its own real presence in the world.'[43] In what ways does the acting subject of the trial scene achieve his own presence in the world? In what way can this particular moment of his history which unmasks and finishes falsehood be said to be present, contemporary? Why must we, if we are to be faithful to the One whose identity is disclosed therein, talk about truth – the truth he is – as eternal and so contemporary? Well, we describe him as contemporary, as present and ministering, because he is eternal. Without talk of truth's identity as eternal, we lose the sense of what is contemporaneity's foundation. 'We cannot begin at a lower level than that of the decree of God's eternal love, in which the Father sent the Son and the Son obeyed the Father...to participate in fellowship with Him and eternal life, by giving Himself to be his Covenant-partner.'[44] It is God's eternal decree that we be his covenant partner. We are recipients of God's eternal love manifest in the Father's sending and the Son's obedience – we whose, like Judas's, 'existence is so diametrically opposite from His own'.[45] The eternal character of God's triune love is the ground for an account of Christ's contemporaneity, because eternal love is the love that *is*. It is not the love of an agent whose love and will are occasioned by circumstances, contingencies of one sort or another. It has, rather, an eternal basis and status. The function of an account of the eternality of Christ's identity is to remind us that he is 'the reflection of the radiance of the eternal mercy in which God willed to take sinful man to Himself, and actually did take him to Himself by the handing-over of His Son'.[46] The 'eternal mercy' of

---

[42] This seems to me to be the essence of Paul's statements in Rom. 9–11. God takes up his own people's disobedience in such a way that their disobedience becomes the means of blessing not only for them but also for the whole of the Gentile world.

[43] *CD* IV/3, 212.

[44] *CD* II/2, 491.

[45] *CD* II/2, 491.

[46] *CD* II/2, 497.

God is radiant. Its contemporary presence in Christ is a function of its eternality. Hence God's eternal mercy endures, it overcomes. The identity of Christ is as the eternal one. He does not become mercy but *is* eternal mercy. And so he overcomes the best of our efforts to extinguish him. They cannot endure because his eternal mercy is forever grounded in God's love whereby the Father sends and the Son is sent in the power of the Spirit. His deity is antecedent and therefore radiant in its triumph over sin and death. His presence just *is* his eternal radiance, the overflow of the love that sends and is sent and, in turn, fills.

Truth, as ingredient in reconciliation, is real and therefore present to the world. Our history is really re-presented to us in Jesus Christ. Sinners that we are, we resonate with the chief priests' insistence to 'have no King but the emperor' (John 19.15). Nonetheless, truth is present as a person whose history gathers up our history, which is really only an extended series of footnotes to the actions of Pilate and the chief priests in the passion history, and in gathering our history up into his, his history 'continually becomes a new reality to His own and to the world'.[47] Truth as a person – the identity of this One – is reality. And reality is, when we peer ahead into John 20, resurrected. Although he rose from the dead 'once', it is because he rose from the dead that his history can 'continually become a new reality'.[48] But reality, in order to become present in the midst of the world, 'attacks the darkness which envelopes and indwells him [humanity] for man's [humanity's] sake, for his good, for his salvation'.[49] In John 18 and 19, the attack comes to a culmination.

The history of Jesus is expansive and inclusive. It includes hypostasized falsehood, Jewish unbelief, Gentile cowardice, triumphing over them by suffering them. In the trial scenes in John's Gospel we are really watching a scene that has been playing itself out since the Garden of Eden. For we want to put God on trial, the Son of God on the defensive – and we do. We want to precede him, not follow. We quite enjoy our pretensions to authority, and are threatened by anyone who calls them into question. In sum, we think it good for us to extinguish the identity of the One who claims to be antecedent

[47] *CD* IV/3, 234.

[48] Barth describes the resurrection in a twofold sense as both a 'coming from' death and a 'going to' heaven. The latter moment is the ascension. But as the ascended one he continues to come to us as one who overcomes death so that we might dwell where he is, at the right hand of the Father.

[49] *CD* IV/3, 251.

to us, a King whose voice is heard by those who belong 'to the truth' (John 18.37). In Webster's words, 'the end of interpretation is hearing the gospel I once hated, but which I must now learn to love; and in this light, I must conduct myself'.[50] We, together with John's inter- locutors, must learn to love what we 'naturally hate'. The way in which we learn to love what we hate is to attend to his history as present and to hear that history as one that includes a command, a law that is good for us. We are to recognize that the eternal outworking of the decree contains particular moral force. Accordingly, an account of the command to truthfulness is necessary, if we are to be caught up in the movement of truth, and to live as those for whom the truth is 'a spiritually visible reality to be seen'.[51]

THE INDICATIVE AND THE IMPERATIVE

The Command of Truth

The language of command demands attention in order to counter any sense that the presence of Christ does not contain within itself an imperative, a 'Do this', law, you might say. In the second part of this chapter, I sought to indicate the identity of Christ as eternal and as such contemporary or present truth, and in the last part I will reflect on the moral significance of the presence of Christ understood as One who leads into the truth. In this section on the command of truth, I account for the way in which Christ's personhood as the presence and the ongoing ministry of truth establishes a people of truth: his personhood as self-involving. The way in which he involves us in himself is his command. Truth is not simply a crisis or an attack, in other words; the truth that is the eternal and contemporary Savior establishes a people of truth. Indeed, he promises to do so. And the instrument by which he establishes a people of truth is the *command* of truth; Truth claims. Christ's self-presentation as the truth makes true. The event that he is, his personhood, is an implicating and creative event. More specifically, it is creative of a people, a congregation. 'As Jesus Christ lives, so he gathers a congregation around himself.'[52]

When it comes to the trial scenes and the crucifixion in John we get a glimpse of this. As the one who is truth lays down his life, he calls from the cross to his mother, saying, ' "Woman, here is your

---

[50] Webster, 'Resurrection and Scripture', in *Christology and Scripture*, 153.

[51] Webster, 'Resurrection and Scripture', in *Christology and Scripture*, 154.

[52] Webster, 'Resurrection and Scripture', in *Christology and Scripture*, 148.

son". Then he said to the disciple, "Here is your mother". And from that hour the disciple took her into his own home' (John 19.26-27). What we observe here is that the disciple whom Jesus loved is now an adopted member of Jesus' family. The disciple who does not do what Peter did – that is, deny – is welcomed into a new family. I point this out because it suggests very much what the presence of Christ's truth accomplishes among us: it creates a new family and adopts us so that we, too, may be part of the family of truth. It generates an audience for itself. The truth is evocative of a new set of relations with new commitments and allegiances.

The language of command, specifically the command to truthfulness, is hardly compelling language to many, however. That Jesus' givenness or factuality, his identity and presence as the truth, is also a *command*, sounds to many today to be rather authoritarian. But again, what kind of command are we talking about? Are we talking about a command that is removed from the person of Christ, or a command that is very much a function of this person's expansiveness, his glory and radiance? I argue that it is the latter, and turn to Bonhoeffer for an account of the salutary function of the language of command, the command of Christ as that which makes true and gathers together a truthful community.

A brief exploration of the theological function of the commandment of God acts as our entry point to the ethical, to explore the way in which the person of Christ is also a law and command. '*The commandment is the sole authorization for ethical discourse*', Bonhoeffer writes.[53] The commandment licenses and evokes ethical discourse because it 'is the total and concrete claim of human beings by the merciful and holy God in Jesus Christ'.[54] The commandment of God is law, insofar as it claims the whole human – the world – for Christ and the truth he is. The commandment is the task that is ingredient in Christ's gift of himself as the truth. It is what 'comes from above to below'.[55] To live as people of the truth is not a capacity we possess in and of ourselves, then. Truth is a person who is present, and present and ministering as one who claims: his presence *is* claim. His presence is a commanding presence.

Were we to command ourselves, we would, as the trial scenes starkly remind us, be quite content to push the Son of God out of

[53] *DBW*, vol. 6, *Ethics*, 378, original emphasis.
[54] *DBW*, vol. 6, *Ethics*, 378.
[55] *DBW*, vol. 6, *Ethics*, 380.

the world. Jesus' answer to Pilate, ' "You would have no power over me unless it had been given you from above" ' (John 19.11), reminds us that the commandment of God has power precisely because it is from above. Ethics, too, proceeds from above, in response to a claim about the way the world is. What we are to do is given to us; ethics is, therefore, not a response to a word that arises from the created world. It proceeds, rather, with attention to all of life as claimed by the One who has power over it. Indeed, there is a great deal of irony in Pilate's second interview with Jesus, because Pilate is really the one who is being judged, even though he acts as judge.[56] He is judged by the One being judged precisely because he is seeking to establish himself as the judge. The law of truth – Christ's personhood – is a not-so-subtle reminder that we are those who are judged by the judge who allows himself to be judged in our place.[57]

This is good news: it means that all of life is subject to a 'clear direction'.[58] That is, 'The commandment of God becomes the daily divine guidance of our lives.'[59] The inhumanity of Pilate's regime and of the chief priests is again resultant from the fact that the latter, especially, has turned the law into a property, a possession – '*we* [emphasis mine] have a law' (John 19.7). The chief priests are no longer students of the law but those who preside over it. 'God's commandment permits human beings to live as human beings *before* [emphasis mine] God – as human beings, not merely as the makers of ethical decisions, as students of ethics.'[60] This is really the dogmatic foundation for any treatment of God's commandment or God's law. God's commandment – the command to live truthfully – is not simply an imperative: it is first expressive of an indicative. That is to say, the commandment establishes human beings in such a way that they may 'be human before God', precisely because we have been made human beings before God in the person of Jesus Christ. The command is the instrument whereby we become and are made to agree with the reality of revelation. The commandment or law of God permits or allows us to become in Christ's hands what we are, namely those who exist in he who *is* 'righteousness (*dikaiosunē*) and sanctification (*hagiasmos*) and redemption (*apolutrōsis*)'.[61] Who are we before God

[56] John 19.8-11.
[57] *CD* IV/1, 211–83.
[58] *DBW*, vol. 6, *Ethics*, 381.
[59] *DBW*, vol. 6, *Ethics*, 381.
[60] *DBW*, vol. 6, *Ethics*, 383.
[61] 1 Cor. 1.30.

but those who are *in* Jesus Christ, in his very person. So the command to be people marked by truth, to be those who listen to Christ's voice, is not one which falls upon us as a raw or naked duty. Instead, the commandment to be truthful before God is soaked in the promise of God present in Christ through Word and Spirit.

That Bonhoeffer uses the language of *being* human before God rather than acting humanly before God indicates the priority which is ascribed to Christ as One in whom we live, move and have our being. The commandment permits or licenses one to act in accord with the very law of our being. As those 'hidden with Christ in God', so too is our obedience to the command; so, too, is ethics.[62] It is bound up with a person – the hypostatic union of God and humanity in him – who wills to achieve his personhood in us. The commandment revealed in Christ is revealed by One who does what he commands, and so too enables us to live as he does in fidelity to the will of his Father even unto death. 'In Jesus Christ human beings are set free to be truly human before God.'[63] Accordingly, the commandment liberates precisely because its humanizing content is Jesus Christ. I would suggest, then, that ethics is evangelical to the extent that it takes seriously the fact that the One whom we are to obey in life and in death is the One in whom we obey and are given the power to obey through the Spirit in life and in death.

Bonhoeffer's account of the command is salutary precisely because of its sheer Christological concentration. Although some worry that Bonhoeffer's use of the language of mandates in relation to the command of God dilutes or lessens the force of this concentration, or, worse, takes attention away from the crisis character of the commandment, a generous reading of the mandates would indicate that this is his way of re-enforcing the commandment of God in the person of Christ as confronting all of life.[64] Indeed, the four mandates (marriage and family, work, government, and church) are 'to be understood simultaneously as the laying claim to, commandeering of, and formation of a certain earthly domain by the divine command'.[65] Mandates language is Bonhoeffer's way of ensuring that the concrete character of the commandment of God is honored. The

---

[62] Col. 3.3.

[63] *DBW*, vol. 6, *Ethics*, 400.

[64] See further my article, ' "The Indivisible Whole of God's Reality": On the Agency of Jesus in Bonhoeffer's *Ethics*', *International Journal of Systematic Theology* 12 (July 2010): 283–301.

[65] *DBW*, vol. 6, *Ethics*, 389.

commandment claims all of life – namely, the mandates – in order that life be lived before God by the power of God. Similarly, Barth: 'I must see my life itself as reached and affected by the command, in the sense that I also see my life-act as such set in the crisis of the command and realize that I myself am responsible for my life-act as such.'[66] All of life is set in the crisis of the command – as such the command is 'an attack on the whole man'. But it is also, suggests Barth, 'a promise for the whole man'.[67] Stated Christologically, Christ mortifies – the attack against the flesh – and vivifies in the Spirit through the promise. Christ not only extinguishes the old Adam but, in extinguishing him, gives rise to the new.

The challenge present in any theologically responsible account of the command of God is to describe well the extent to which God's command as the law of Christ is both attack or crisis *and* promise. God's command is an attack on the denial that creaturely life's 'factuality has a significance'.[68] All of Bonhoeffer's talk about 'this-worldliness' in the prison letters is an amplification of this theme. The notion that reconciliation takes us away from this world, rather than directing us toward it, is a footnote to the basic truth that this world and not another is subject to God's reconciliation – the revelation of reconciliation – in Christ effective through the Spirit. The command of truth is a command that would have us see the human being(s) before us as located in the same person we are. That Pilate cannot hear the King who is before him, that he cannot understand what he says, ' "Here is your King!" ' is precisely because he is deaf to the absolutely *other* life that is before him and that in a sense includes him (John 19.14). Such deafness is what the command of God – the command of truth – attacks and heals because it grants by the power of the Spirit ears with which to hear.

'The factuality of an alien life…is to be respected for the Creator's sake.'[69] In other words, the commandment of God renders us our brother's and sister's keeper, precisely because we know how God in the person of Christ holds them and us too. This is the command of truth. The commandment of God brings us into the realm of 'responsibility' for one another. 'True fear of God and true morality begin when in the light of God's compensating justice I and my

[66] Karl Barth, *Ethics* (Edinburgh: T&T Clark, 1978), 124.

[67] Barth, *Ethics*, 119.

[68] Barth, *Ethics*, 139.

[69] Barth, *Ethics*, 143.

righteousness are also on the scales and my righteousness might prove to be filthy rags in which I have wrapped myself so as not to have to be my brother's keeper.'[70] The commandment of truth renders us our brother's keeper. We are not our brother's keeper out of a sense of duty. We are, rather, by the commandment – most especially the commandment's content, the person of Christ – freed *for* our brother or sister, free to venture action that rests solely on our responsibility for him or her. But again, our responsibility towards his or her (community) is not our concern in isolation from Jesus Christ. In Christ the whole of humanity is accepted, judged and awakened to new life by God in him through the agency of the Spirit. This is humanity's form and that to which it is to be conformed. 'The real human being is allowed to be in freedom the creature of the Creator. To be conformed with the one who became human means that we may be the human beings we really are… God changes God's form into human form in order that human beings can become, not God, but human before God.'[71] The commandment of truth is that of simply living humanly before God in the person and thus presence of God's Son. We do not live before God in isolation from God. Ethics is evangelical inasmuch as it not only takes seriously the person of the God-man, but also he as One whose personhood is expansive in such a way as to summon 'a community into being', gathering 'it around his commanding presence' and 'direct[ing] it to hear and obey him'.[72]

An account of the commandment – or law – of God is really good news then. It is not one step removed from the Gospel. The Gospel indeed announces that 'Jesus Christ is our human response to God'.[73] Because he is this, he is as such our obedience to God. He is revelation *and* response. That we are called to be people of truth, to live truthfully, which is to hear his voice and to behold him as King, is quite possible because he is 'the man' (John 19.5). That is to say, he is the one who represents us and is our substitute before God as the obedient man. To think that ethics – obedience to the commandment – could be undertaken apart from deploying an account of Christ's incarnation and atonement, as Torrance reminds

[70] Barth, *Ethics*, 171.
[71] *DBW*, vol. 6, *Ethics*, 92, 96.
[72] Webster, 'Resurrection and Scripture', in *Christology and Scripture*, 149.
[73] Thomas F. Torrance, *The Mediation of Christ*, rev. ed. (Colorado Springs, CO: Helmers & Howard, 1992), 80.

us, is most problematic. When we talk about the human response
to God – which is ethics – we do not leave Christology behind. The
thesis of this essay is that ethics is underwritten by Christology (and
soteriology), and that evangelical ethics is, more specifically, ethics
that is circumscribed by and located within Christ as the One who
obeys for us, and who is always what we are to be and gives through
his Spirit the power to be what we are to be. In other words, ethics
proceeds 'from the side of God and from the side of man'.[74] Christ
is the One in whom there is no gap between is and ought; he acts as
he is. So when language of substitute and representative is deployed
in ethics, it is to remind us that another precedes our frail acts of
obedience and includes us in his obedience. Indeed, Christ Jesus is
the one whose faithfulness is substituted in the place of our faithlessness; Christ Jesus is the one who represents us before the Father as
one in whom our ostensible obedience is sanctified such that it truly
becomes the obedience of faith.[75]

The Imitation of Truth

The language of imitation is best considered when it is taken up with
reference to the hypostatic union. To be sure, St. Paul in Ephesians
5.1 would have us 'be imitators of God, as beloved children, and live
in love, as Christ loved us'. The language of imitation is language
which presupposes that there is One in advance of us to imitate. We
are to imitate Jesus Christ as our human response to God. Not only
does he imitate God, he is God the Son; his work, his life, his acts are
entirely transparent to his person, his being. His work is a function
of his person. If we are 'in Christ', we are in God, and so we live and
obey on the basis of our being in him. We do not imitate a model or
a pattern but rather a person who lives, whose presence 'humanizes',
who is the active agent in shaping us in accord with his pattern.[76]

Accordingly, the command to truthfulness is a command that does
not originate from an agent from the past. 'It [the ascension] is his
withdrawal in his mode of physical presence in order to be with us in
his mode of universal presence through word and Spirit.'[77] Christ is
present through the work of the Spirit sanctifying men and women
such that they may live transparently to his presence, his 'word of

---

[74] Torrance, *Atonement*, 44.
[75] See Gal. 2.20.
[76] Torrance, *Mediation*, 72.
[77] Walker, Introduction to Torrance, *Atonement*, lxviii.

truth, the gospel of your salvation' (Eph. 1.13). In Webster's words, 'The presence of his is not merely an additional factor alongside all other determinants, but rather that which conditions all creaturely time and space. Temporal existence is existence in his presence, *coram Christo.*'[78] So we imitate Christ, to be sure, as one whose response to his Father is appropriated to us through the Spirit, and given an audience in the Christian community. We truly obey his person, his command of truth – to live transparently to his voice – when we recognize that he fulfills the truth from our side and also God's side. Ethics understood as obedience to the truth is a light yoke. It is really the attempt to expand conceptually what Jesus claims in John 14.10: 'I am in the Father, and you in me, and I in you.' It is to take the hypostatic union as the beginning, middle and end point of ethics.

Ethics in the presence of Jesus is ethics in accord with his promeity. The eternal Christ who is our contemporary is profoundly for us. To be sure, this is a Bonhoefferian theme:

> Our relationship to God is no 'religious' relationship to some highest, most powerful, and best being imaginable – that is not genuine transcendence. Instead, our relationship to God is a new life in 'being there for others', through participation in the being of Jesus... God in human form!... 'the human being for others'! therefore the Crucified One. The human being living out of the transcendent.[79]

Jesus in his very being *is* the man for others. To live in Christ is to exist for others, which is to participate in the form of Jesus' existence.

What Bonhoeffer says about Christ's promeity is indeed salutary, but I would suggest that it needs to be supplemented by Torrance's simple point that Jesus is also our human response to God: his life of fidelity to his Father's will is ingredient in his promeity. The command of truth, the command to live truthfully, is to live transparently to the Word whose being for us claims us. The person and presence of truth renders us as those who exist for others. But the Christ who *is* for others, is the Christ who fulfills for and in us what his very being demands of us. In other words, the gathered community becomes a community for others 'in the power of his achievement'.[80]

The command of truth contains an audacious promise. Christ promises his followers that his fulfillment of what he commands is, in the Spirit, their own; his merits are brought home to us through the

---

[78] Webster, 'Resurrection and Scripture', in *Christology and Scripture*, 147.
[79] *DBW*, vol. 8, *Letters and Papers*, 501.
[80] Webster, 'Resurrection and Scripture', in *Christology and Scripture*, 153.

Spirit in faith as sealed by the sacraments. What Torrance's profound point teaches is that the command of God in Christ – the command to truthfulness – is fulfilled. It is a *fait accompli*. We participate in the One who is truly for us, but whose promeity comes with very real and serious content, namely that he does for us what he commands and so includes us through his Spirit in his obedience. This is the way in which his person is *pro nobis*. He is personally present in a mode appropriate to his ascended state, a mode that is utterly creative. He not only *clarifies* but creates *ex nihilo* people of truth on the basis of his response for us and in our place.[81]

It follows, then, that the command or law of God is ingredient in the Gospel of God. The law that we live under is this: that what God has commanded of us is indeed fulfilled in the person of his Son present to us in the Spirit. In him we are what we ought to be: children of God. Or, to cast the discussion in terms of justification and sanctification, 'Christ...attaches himself to us [the reality of justification] in order to gives us those new dispositions of attachment to him [the reality of sanctification].'[82] The command of God which sanctifies does not fall with a thud then upon us. It too is a radical gift, for its content and achievement, its inner law, is Christ. Ethical acts are acts transparent to the command of God which always places us before the Son of God. The command is simply the word of the King, the instrument whereby we are exhorted to honor Pilate's words to the Jews, 'Here is your King!' (John 19.14)

Commandment language is covenantal language. Exodus 20.16 reads, 'You shall not bear false witness against your neighbour.' But this is of course precisely what the chief priests do. Again, they exclaim, 'We have no king but the emperor' (John 19.15). They do not do what the law would have them do, which is to acknowledge the truthfulness of Pilate's declaration, 'Here is your King.' When reading the Gospels, in this case, John, we are not only read by them or absorbed by them; more than that, we are to read them in such a way that we understand ourselves to be *in* their principal actor or agent. In other words, we don't read of a history that is far removed from us and our feeble attempts to obey. We read, rather, of a history that is not simply for others, but one in which we and indeed all people are radically implicated, one in which we are. The radicality of Paul's dictum 'in Christ' and the profound inner unity that exists

---

[81] See further Krötke, *Gottes Klarheiten*, 121–59.
[82] Tanner, *Christ the Key*, 92.

between John's Gospel (and the Synoptics) in relation to Paul is just this: that when we read the Gospel, when we see faithfulness to the Father's will enacted by his Son even unto death, we see our response – indeed, what was commanded of us – taking place. It is not enough to say that Jesus is for me; what needs to be said is that the trial scenes and subsequent crucifixion *include* me, indeed all of humanity, for in them we encounter one who responds to God in our place as our substitute and representative. Peter, the chief priests (and the Jews), and Pilate, too, are us. To be sure, they are particular Jewish and Gentile figures in history; but the trial scenes in all of their particularity stand for something far more general as they represent the fullness of the first Adam's fallenness. But the second Adam is there too, and we see him respond to our assaults in a manner that undoes – better, finishes – those assaults. We see in Christ God's response to ourselves. If Jesus is our human response to God, then the trial scenes do not merely read us; they place us too, insofar as the response to us that Jesus gives is now ours too, vicariously so. We respond to our sin in him; and we obey his command in him. The nothingness in us is assaulted by him. Indeed, in him we are victorious over the nothingness that will take his life because our faith and obedience are ultimately his.

If ethics is truly *in* the presence of Jesus Christ, then it is present in all the moments of his life, his death, resurrection, ascension and heavenly session. They are all relevant. This chapter is an attempt to demonstrate how one moment of his life, namely his passion (the trial scenes) is not simply a negative moment for ethics, for human response. It contains a profoundly positive moment too, a Yes. The Son of God goes to trial so that we might not have to go to trial. Indeed, we are tried in him and not found wanting. Obedience to the command of truth – the command to live transparently to Christ, then – engenders human response. Our acts of faith, our ethics, if you will, have no independent existence. They are always taken up into all the moments of Christ's history. The trial scenes demonstrate that no one belongs to the truth; Jews and Gentiles are likewise apostate and estranged from the truth. And yet, within that No, the harsh word that we do not belong, there is a Yes. We do belong to the truth and listen to his voice because all of the moments of his life belong to us by the faith he gives through the Spirit. Ethics *in* the presence of Christ is ethics in him, his whole human life which is one of 'saving significance'.[83]

The further one penetrates into this holy mystery, the greater the disparity between the ought and the is, the commanding presence of Christ. To be taken captive by Christ's presence, which is really the only theological function of commandment language in the Bible, is not to be taken captive by an idea but by a person, specifically *all* the moments of his personhood. This is not to suggest a Christomonism, but rather to suggest that every event, every moment of this life, is relevant to us, for we are, as his gathered people, *in* each moment. If a person – Jesus Christ – is their history, then all the moments of their history matter. To be sure, there is an eschatological reserve in all of this. 'On that day', says Jesus, 'you will know that I am in my Father, and you in me, and I in you' (John 14.20). And yet, the knowledge of faith has already a share in what will be revealed and is being revealed. Ethics is Christian to the extent that it is taken captive by *all* the moments of a life that taken together are the Gospel of our salvation. If Bonhoeffer is right in affirming that 'the same God who makes us to live in the world without the working hypothesis of God is the God before whom we stand continually', then the Christ who goes to 'trial' before both Pilate and the chief priests is the Christ who lets humans continue to try him even though he has already been tried, who uses that very trial to end all trials of himself.[84] He allows himself to be pushed out, and pushed out he is, but that is the way in which he helps us. In this next and last section, I will reflect on the moral and pastoral significance of this. What are some of the moral and pastoral particulars ingredient in an account of Christ as eternal and so contemporary and presently ministering as the truth? What might some of the moral dimensions particular to such an account be?

THE MORAL SIGNIFICANCE OF TRUTH

Having described the eternal and contemporary character of truth on the basis of John's witness to the truth and the commandment ingredient in it, what follows in this section is a reflection on what can be said about the particular moral significance of the presence of Christ the truth.[85] The language of presence is, as I have been arguing, quite

---

[83] Walker, Introduction to Torrance, *Atonement*, lxxv.

[84] *DBW*, vol. 8, *Letters and Papers*, 479.

[85] Just as O'Donovan asks after 'what can be said for the *particular* significance of the

important theologically: it reminds us that what is reality – namely, Christ's self-presentation and identification in John's narrative as *the* truth – includes and encompasses also the subjective. Indeed, it grounds, forms and perfects our life in the truth here and now. That is to say, the truth that is Christ is wide-ranging and far-reaching and as such it takes up the question of existence and of ethics, precisely because it is a matter of what *is*: the being of the person of the Christ who is present. Christ's presence is not therefore an accompanying presence. He is not a chaplain. Rather, Christ is present in such a way as to evoke activity that is correspondent to and participant in what he as the truth is and is now doing.

As the last section discussed, he draws us into his sphere, his field via his command. His command is the instrument he uses to align us to his presence and activity, his person. 'Everyone who belongs to the truth (*alētheias*) listens (*akouei*) to my voice' (John 18.37). But one last thing needs to be addressed, namely reflection on the moral and pastoral import and particulars of the presence of Christ, he who is now present in his person via his command. In order to provide a responsible reflection, it would be good to proceed by engaging O'Donovan's classic work *Resurrection and Moral Order: An Outline for Evangelical Ethics*. O'Donovan argues therein that Christian ethics has an objective reference. That is, the human is to live his or her life in accordance with the order God has given to creation. O'Donovan writes, 'The order of things that God has made is *there*. It is objective, and mankind has a place within it. Christian ethics, therefore, has an objective reference because it is concerned with man's life in accordance with this order.'[86] To be sure, the truthful life is life in accord with an order, the order being the command of Christ which is to hear his voice. Although I have used the language of presence, presence language is but another way of stating the order in which we live, move, and have our being. Having said that, the language of 'presence' does better theological work than the language of 'order', precisely because the objective reference point in ethics *is* the person

---

resurrection', so I want to ask after what can be said for the particular significance of the presence of Christ's truth. See *Resurrection and Moral Order*, ix, original emphasis.

[86] O'Donovan, *Resurrection and Moral Order*, 17, original emphasis. I have to wonder whether creation at times usurps the place of Christology in O'Donovan's text. In particular, the language of covenant and its necessary correlate election seem to be displaced. Is creation 'the "presupposition" of history?' That said, creation as the presupposition of history does not receive its *telos* from history but rather 'from that one saving event'. Ibid., 62, 66.

of Jesus Christ, a person whose presence, whose very liveliness, is a function of his identity as One who is at work ministering. Or again, the objective reference point for ethics is a person who is present and as such active in making us participant by the Spirit in his presence, his ministry.

This, it seems to me, is the best way to honor the importance of the presence of Jesus for ethics. Ethics is indeed premised upon an order. But that order *is* Jesus' history which is present. 'The risen one suffers no hindrance.'[87] To live ethically is to live in light of his present, to be transformed by his presence. That is to say, the identity of this one as the truth is One whose presence is generative of a response. And that response, that corollary, is ethics. The response, freely undertaken, has, moreover, a reality of its own in that it is not coerced but rather takes place as simply thanksgiving and obedience. The response is neither 'at ontological parity with the divine' nor independent of 'the divine from first to last'.[88] Instead, the response is to the present and ministering Christ. And so, with O'Donovan, I wholeheartedly concur that 'morality must respond to the agency of God in history'.[89] But moving beyond O'Donovan, I want to talk about moral agency in a more explicitly Christological fashion than does he, specifically with respect to the identity of Jesus which is not only coterminous with his presence but also with his ministry, all of which has serious pastoral significance.

To O'Donovan's credit, he does not reify the created moral order. In an important statement he writes, 'True knowledge of the moral order is knowledge "in Christ".'[90] Christ is the order of creation. The moral order, of which O'Donovan makes much, has explicitly Christological content. That said, O'Donovan's treatment of the moral order itself does not always adequately or consistently honor his own best insights. For O'Donovan: 'Morality is man's participation in the created order. Christian morality is his glad response to the deed of God which has restored, proved and fulfilled that order making man free to conform to it.'[91] I would rather one say that Christian morality is the human person's response to the identity of Christ who is as this One present, and as the present One ministering

[87] Webster, 'Resurrection and Scripture', in *Christology and Scripture*, 140.
[88] O'Donovan, *Resurrection and Moral Order*, 34.
[89] O'Donovan, *Resurrection and Moral Order*, 36.
[90] O'Donovan, *Resurrection and Moral Order*, 85.
[91] O'Donovan, *Resurrection and Moral Order*, 76.

and thereby effecting participation in what he *is* doing – in this case, witnessing to the truth he is, conforming us to what he is: the truth. This, I think, is ingredient in what has been said thus far. Truth is 'outgoing, and therefore eloquent'.[92] And because it is this, there is a sense in which its significance will be new each and every day.

Bonhoeffer's distrust of 'inwardness' or 'subjectivity' in ethics and in church life in general is because it renders response to the truth a staid enterprise. Ethics conceived inwardly could never become 'guilty' before the good, because the good was forever immanently conceived. The good became a matter of doing what is available to me or to us. The same can be said of truth. What is necessary is a hearing of the truth as that which is to be obeyed, followed *after*. Jesus Christ is to be heard, precisely because he can never be identified with 'our projects'. Hence we have truth's morally significant character. This Bonhoeffer 'gets' when it comes to describing his rationale for participation in the conspiracy to assassinate Hitler. Bonhoeffer never argues, for example, that either his or his co-conspirators' conduct was truthful action. Rather, he knows that there was guilt involved, that, plainly and simply, he and his co-conspirators were rendering themselves guilty with respect to the command of God to 'not murder', and in so doing they had to but throw themselves into the arms of God (Exod. 20.13).[93] Herein Bonhoeffer provides great insight into our situation: the gathered community is to do likewise. It is to hear, and to act as it hears and so trust that its hearing of what it once hated is embraced by the truth, he who is ever so graciously grounding and perfecting his truth among us such that we may be its audience, and so be acted upon in order that we may in the Spirit live in him who is 'infinitely alive and ceaselessly at work'.[94]

The benefits of Jesus Christ's faithfulness to the will of his Father even unto death are those in which Christians participate by faith, in short his merits. Ethics, therefore, is not so much oriented to an order – even if that order is understood to be 'in Christ' – but rather is orientated to the person of Christ himself. Ethics is about being oriented to an agent and even more so to an order whose history is present, whose agency is reality. The moral import and significance of

---

[92] Webster, 'Resurrection and Scripture', in *Christology and Scripture*, 141.

[93] See further *DBW*, vol. 6, *Ethics*, 297. The freedom Christ grants sanctifies the law, even as it may require the breaking of the law.

[94] Webster, 'Resurrection and Scripture', in *Christology and Scripture*, 149.

the trial scene is that the Christ who is on trial is a Christ who in being on trial puts us – his hearers, his gathered community – on trial. We are as it were absorbed into his trial. The trial is being played out before us, unmasking our false pretensions with respect to his truth and our moral laxity in relationship to it.

If that is so, the basic problematic that lies behind O'Donovan's construal, is, I would suggest, his account of the objective and the subjective. What is, for O'Donovan, objective is the moral order of creation. It is to this that human life is to be directed and conformed. Yet such knowledge of the moral order is found in Christ; the 'redeemed creation' is identical to the risen and ascended Christ, who is the firstborn of the new humanity. When it comes to the subjective, however, it is the Spirit who 'makes the reality of redemption distant from us in time, both *present* and *authoritative*'.[95] What I want to suggest is that reconciliation – and redemption as its culmination – is present and active: the Spirit does not extend Christ so much as enable participation in him. In Barth's words,

> 'Jesus Christ lives' means that his history takes place today in the same way as did that yesterday – indeed, as the same history. Jesus Christ speaks and acts and rules – it all means that this history is present. In other words, when we say that Jesus Christ is in every age, we say that his history takes place in every age. He is this *operatio*, this event.[96]

In describing the claim that 'Jesus lives', Barth, like O'Donovan, establishes an account of the relationship between the objective and the subjective. However, Barth includes a motif that O'Donovan elides. Indeed, Barth is at pains to point out in the above quote's context that this history does take place in and through and by the Spirit. Christ unites us to himself and thus to his history by his Spirit. That is, Christ's history – the history in which he is – is not 'distant from us in time'. To be the One he is, is to be present to us and thus to our times. The Spirit is not so much, for Barth, the mode of being God who authoritatively presents Christ to us. Rather, the Spirit enables us to participate, to be transformed in accord with him whose identity is as One who is savingly and transformingly present: 'I am coming to you' (John 14.18). Barth has a pneumatology, as does O'Donovan. But Barth's pneumatology is somewhat different, for it is premised upon a differently inflected Christology. Indeed, for Barth Christ does not need to be made present: our times are neither by the Spirit nor the

---

[95] O'Donovan, *Resurrection and Moral Order*, 102, original emphasis.
[96] *CD* IV/2, 107.

church made present to his time. Rather, Christ's time, the time of his first coming, is present by the Spirit in a manner that anticipates the time of his advent coming. The Spirit, accordingly, is the mode of being of the risen and ascended one among us, the person of God who works to enlighten hearts and minds in order that we be drawn into Christ's presence and continuing ministry, into faithful hearing of his voice. The Spirit's drawing is effective, such that we can correspond in word and deed to Christ, and so become transparent to what he is doing. 'The Spirit is the bond by which Christ effectually unites himself to us.'[97] In short, the Spirit is the person of God who fosters transformation in accord with the presence and ministry of Jesus Christ, who as the One he is, is present and at work, redemptively so.

In a section on the significance of Christ's truth, the Spirit ought not to suffer neglect. Rather, the Spirit is one who effects personal and corporate (eschatological) participation in the Christ who is our contemporary, whose history lives, transformingly so. Indeed, it is we who are so very often distant from Christ, not he from us. Jesus is active, and it is the Spirit who is the power of his activity, his contemporaneity. What lies behind O'Donovan's account is, I suspect, the worry that Barth does not give us enough support as regards the moral complexities facing us. Precisely because Barth does not adequately differentiate the ontological and the epistemological, and therefore repudiates certain aspects of the doctrine of creation, he champions, according to O'Donovan, 'a formal account of the theological basis of ethics which, depending exclusively on the divine command – interpreted in the existentialist way as particular and unpredictable – was far too thin to support the extensive responsibility for moral deliberation which he would claim in practice and sometimes even defend in theory'.[98]

There is a misunderstanding here, I think. Barth's account of the divine command is not quite as 'unpredictable' as O'Donovan suggests, even though his comment is directed to Barth's less Christologically concentrated *Ethics* of the early 1930s. The command of God, as Barth understands it, does support 'extensive responsibility for moral deliberation' precisely because it is a

---

[97] John Calvin, *Institutes of the Christian Religion*, ed. John T. McNeill (Philadelphia: Westminster Press, 1965), III.I.1.

[98] O'Donovan, *Resurrection and Moral Order*, 87. This is of course a worry of Bonhoeffer's, too. In *Letters and Papers*, his critique of Barth is that Barth's theology tells us how things are, but provides us with scant resources for how to live in accord with how things are.

concrete command which is spoken by One who is our contemporary, whose history is present, who summons obedience in accord with his proclamation of his history which, by the power of the Spirit, never returns without effect. Moral deliberation does not take place for Barth in a vacuum, in a place removed from the identity of the One whose presence is also a participatory summons. The summons that Jesus Christ is, is a consequence of the ongoing and dynamic activity of his ascension as One whose history is operative and present, whose history wills to win among us, in all of the details of life, a human Yes. Ethics does not for Barth depend exclusively on the divine command. The divine command is certainly ethics' form and content, but it is the command of a person, an agent whose identity is as one who is present, whose presence is his history which takes place in every age, whose history contains an *imperative* which is always concrete, because he *is* concrete: 'Here is the man; Here is your King' (John 19.5, 14). Ethics is simply activity undertaken in response to the man who presents himself through the proclamation of those appointed, called and commissioned to proclaim him as a King who would have us live as his people in his world, the world for and to whom he is present in the mode of promise.

Bonhoeffer very much provides a remedy for what ails O'Donovan's account by describing the presence of Christ as the presence of a contemporary, one who as our contemporary does not simply stand beside us but rather actively *forms* us into people of truth. Such formation is rather unpredictable at times. To draw from Kathryn Tanner, human being and by extension 'the material world itself is plastic'; that is to say, open to divine influence.[99] In his *Ethics* manuscript, 'Ethics as Formation', Bonhoeffer describes Christ as one whose form – which includes 'the whole of humanity' – effects formation (that is, ethics). 'Formation occurs only by being drawn into the form of Jesus Christ, by *being conformed to the unique form of the one who became human, was crucified, and is risen*... Christ remains the only one who forms.'[100] Christ's formative work is in the present tense. It is the sense of Christ as one who exists in the present tense that is missing in its fullness from O'Donovan's proposal. For Bonhoeffer, Christ *is* the active agent, the one who forms human beings in accord with his form, that is, 'the human being, accepted, judged, and

---

[99] See Tanner, *Christ the Key*, 52.
[100] *DBW*, vol. 6, *Ethics*, 93, original emphasis.

awakened to new life by God'.[101] The objective is present fostering subjective participation in itself. Christ is contemporary to us, asking us, just as the woman asked Peter, whether we are really one of his disciples.[102]

Christ testifies 'to the truth' and he continues to do so (John 18.37). He is present in the Spirit as the witness who points us to himself. Stated differently, the presence of the Son is also the will of God. 'Now, therefore, we hold forth faith to be a knowledge of God's *will* [emphasis mine] toward us, perceived from his Word.'[103] To know the Word, to know the person of the Word, is to know his will which implicates us in his person. To be a person or community of truth, then, is to listen to his testimony which is not 'from this world' (John 18.36). If it were from this world, it would have perished; but because it is 'from above', it lives and is present to us as an imperative. 'Everyone who belongs to the truth listens to my voice' (John 18.37). Herein lies truth's moral significance.

Such an account, I would argue, docs provide 'extensive resources for moral deliberation'. The 'resources' occur in relation to a creaturely act: hearing. To be sure, the hearing of the truth is unpredictable. But its very unpredictability is rooted in a profound concreteness. That concreteness is his history which takes place in every age. And, as we saw in the previous section, there lies in that history a command. The history itself is a command. So the moral significance of truth is that it is unpredictable – or better, *eschatological* in nature. Thus it is that which is to be heard, followed after, believed. Moral deliberation that allows itself to be interrupted by the history that lives is at the same time capacitated and sustained as *moral* deliberation. The moral significance of truth is that its uncatchableness is generative of concreteness. Its uncatchable character – its presence as spiritually discerned in Word and Spirit – is what gives rise to extensive deliberation as deliberation that is fundamentally hearing, a looking forward to the final manifestation of the advent presence of Christ here and now.

One finds another ally in articulating an account of truth's significance in classical Reformed treatments of Christ's states of exinanition and exaltation, wherein one recognizes how important it is for the Reformed – in opposition to their Lutheran interlocutors'

---

[101] *DBW*, vol. 6, *Ethics*, 92.
[102] See John 18.17.
[103] Calvin, *Institutes*, III.II.6.

embrace of the ubiquity of the body of the risen Christ – to preserve the humanity of the risen, ascended and exalted Christ, and how his exalted humanity bears a certain human response and significance in the here and now. It is important to listen to them, neglected though they may be, for in their rejection of the claim that Christ is indeed present in many places simultaneously, they encourage us to take up another important aspect of the moral significance of Christ's presence. To affirm that the event that he is, his identity, history and ministry is present, is not to suggest that he is not *humanly* present, that the integrity of his glorified humanity is not intact. In this regard, Amandus Polanus writes,

> All these [physical infirmities] he simply set aside, so that he is no longer liable to them. The second part is the glorification of the human nature in both body and soul. Christ's body is rendered glorious, so that it is and remains eternally incorruptible, impassible, immortal, increased in strength and agility, *glowing with brightness and glory heavenly and divine* [emphasis mine], i.e., with the appropriate body of God... But although they [the endowments of both Christ's body and soul] are above nature, they yet are not *counter to nature* [emphasis mine], and they do not remove or destroy the attributes and essentials of human and created nature in order that our flesh and David's seed may reign in heavenly glory for ever.[104]

Polanus makes the important point that the resurrected Jesus remains essentially human. Therefore he cannot be in many places simultaneously, for to be such would be to compromise the integrity of his humanity; it would run counter to nature. I want to affirm with Polanus and also the *Leiden Synopsis* that the presence of the resurrected Jesus is not a presence which dilutes its local character. To be sure, the ascended and exalted Christ is not only present at the right hand of the Father, which is royal or kingly but also priestly imagery, but also as one present at the right hand of the Father he is present in such a way that befits the 'body of God'. That means that there is a range and significance to his risen, ascended and exalted body – 'glowing with brightness and glory heavenly and divine' – that renders it present to us. Indeed, the radiance of Jesus' presence is a function of his identity as the eternal Son.

In this connection, Wollebius writes, 'The exaltation of the person of the God-man belongs to both natures.'[105] So his humanity as with his divinity is exalted. It is proper to Christ's divine nature to be

---

[104] Cited in Heinrich Heppe, *Reformed Dogmatics: Set out and Illustrated from the Sources* (London: George Allen & Unwin, 1950), 496.

[105] Cited in Heppe, *Reformed Dogmatics*, 495.

present to all of our contexts in a manner befitting the glorified nature of his humanity. That Christ is, according to his divine nature, present to our contexts is not to move in the Lutheran direction of ubiquity as regards his resurrected and glorified body but rather to introduce a pneumatological moment. The ascended and exalted Jesus is our contemporary, is transformingly present as the man he is, in and through the power of the Spirit who is the mode of his presence among us. 'Christ in you, the hope of glory (*ē elpis tes doxes*)' (Col. 1.27). The 'you (*umin*)' here is plural, meaning that the community (which includes Gentiles) is implied rather than the individual. Christ is indeed in 'you'; but he is in you, the gathered community by the Holy Spirit. The Holy Spirit is the mode of Christ's exalted presence among us. Stated differently, the ascension denotes the 'mode of [Christ's] *universal* [emphasis mine] presence'.[106] 'Christ is himself present in the work of the Spirit' and is therefore present universally.[107]

The risen and ascended Christ is present, present 'in the Spirit'. He is present in a fashion which befits and honors both his human and divine nature. Douglas Farrow writes, 'What Christ is in the resurrection he must already be in his earthly life; what he is in his earthly life, he must be and remain in his resurrection and ascension.'[108] The risen Jesus is, in his divinity, effusive and bright; he shines as the One he is, One who summons us to participate and be gathered up into the shining of his light. But he does so as one who is human. His exalted humanity shines and is luminous. And his exalted humanity is his earthly humanity 'glowing with brightness and glory heavenly and divine'. It is this brightness that funds the resources necessary, I would argue, for extensive moral deliberation. It is always – often unpredictably – engendering secular parables or analogues to itself. What grounds deliberation, and enables us to handle the details of the moral life responsibly, is the shining of his earthly life, effusive as it is.

Even though the trial scenes in John's Gospel end in crucifixion, Mary Magdalene, on the first day of the week, 'saw that the stone had been removed from the tomb' (John 20.1). Death cannot hold him. The truth that he is shines forth from the tomb, triumphing over the grave. The trial scenes live because he as their subject does, for his

---

[106] Walker, Introduction to Torrance, *Atonement*, lxviii.

[107] Walker, Introduction to Torrance, *Atonement*, lvi.

[108] Douglas Farrow, 'Karl Barth on the Ascension: An Appreciation and Critique', *International Journal of Systematic Theology* 12.2 (2000): 135.

risen and ascended body glows through the Spirit with brightness and glory. It shines; he is luminosity itself. The moral significance of his identity as eternal and contemporary, as the God-man, is that he shines, and in so doing renders us participant in his shining: he is raised from the grave, and in being raised raises us too.

Farrow's helpful piece on the relationship between resurrection and ascension advances classical Reformed insights regarding the brightness and glory of the ascended Christ and therefore offers further resources for an account of the moral significance of his presence and ongoing ministry. In his important article 'Karl Barth on the Ascension: An Appreciation and Critique', he writes that for Barth Jesus' 'ascension concerns the divine Yes to humanity that is realized in him... [and] is that which introduces motion and direction towards God as the proper basis and qualification of human being'.[109] This is a helpful description of how Christ is present with brightness and glory so as to move us toward his glory and thus the truth that he is. For Barth, the ascended Christ is not inert. Rather, as the person he is, he is active and significantly so, effecting 'motion' toward his Father, motion which constitutes the proper basis for human existence. He is presently active as our 'King' and as 'the man'. However, as the ascended one, he generates motion toward his Father and thus toward himself as a function of 'the act which he *is*'.[110] He is his history which radiates forth. We thus live, following Kierkegaard, 'with the situation of contemporaneity'.[111] This is the moral significance of Christ's identity as the truthful one. Extensive moral resources are generated by the new situation, the situation of contemporaneity in which we live.

Farrow argues, further, that Barth's account of contemporaneity, of the ascended one as 'the Contemporary of all men', is indeed 'what the resurrection and ascension disclose, and in disclosing render *effective* [emphasis mine]'.[112] However, Farrow's reading of Barth, and his account of Barth's dependence on Kierkegaard, are helpful

---

[109] Farrow, 'Karl Barth on the Ascension', 132.

[110] Farrow, 'Karl Barth on the Ascension', 135.

[111] Søren Kierkegaard, *Søren Kierkegaard's Journals and Papers* (Bloomington, IN: Indiana University Press, 1967–78), 2:2004, quoted in Farrow, 'Karl Barth on the Ascension', 136. 'He [Jesus] is not resting on high, but he is working, is occupied and concerned with drawing all to himself... Thus, invisible on high, he is also present everywhere, occupied with drawing all to himself.' Søren Kierkegaard, *Practice in Christianity* (Princeton, NJ: Princeton University Press, 1991), 155.

[112] *CD* I/2, 45; and Farrow, 'Karl Barth on the Ascension', 136–37.

– but only to a point, I would argue. The 'one crucial function of the contemporaneity doctrine is to insist that the truth of Jesus [the truth which Jesus *is*] does not need to be filled out, or confirmed by, the content or truth of subsequent history; it is already final'.[113] To be sure, the contemporaneity doctrine bespeaks the sufficiency of what Christ has done as concerns the reconciliation of humankind, its specific unsubstitutability. But there is more to be said. Barth in *CD* IV/3 §69 is always sure to emphasize that Christ does not will to be the truth that he is, or to have his history, apart from us. Christ's identity includes the apostolate as One who 'indefatigably continues to gather, uphold, and send many (or all) others by including them in his appointment, calling, and commission of the Twelve'.[114]

In sum, moral deliberation, if it be truly moral, is anchored in hope. We deliberate in hope because our deliberations are, we pray, subject to the promise of Another to be present to us in a constitutive way. Economic, environmental and social issues need to be elucidated with respect to an ontology that informs us as to what is going on, and through Word and Spirit have given us resources so that we might act in ways commensurate with what is going on. Moral deliberation, if it be moral, is anchored by the hope that what is going on will become manifest to and present in all.

CONCLUSION

To conclude, the moral significance of truth lies in our being included in a concrete presence, the presence of One who invokes inclusion in himself via including us in the apostolate. We are conformed to the spiritually present Christ inasmuch as we hear and obey the testimony which is his. Through their testimony we are gathered to Christ, to his history, and upheld and sent out in his name to bear witness to his history as not only contemporary but coming again. According to Barth:

> The divine 'tradition' which the Church of Jesus Christ proclaims in its confession is the hope of Israel, the promise of its election, which always outlasts and excels and surpasses its rejection... That is what the elect of the

[113] Farrow, 'Karl Barth on the Ascension', 137 n. 43. Likewise, Jesus Christ does not need to be filled out by the church. 'The church does not complete the life of the risen one, as if it were extending it to its furthest reach.' Webster, 'Resurrection and Scripture', in *Christology and Scripture*, 149.

[114] David E. Demson, *Karl Barth and Hans Frei: Different Ways of Reading Scripture* (Grand Rapids, MI: Eerdmans, 1997), 48.

NT are – rejected men elected in and from their rejection, men in whom Judas lives, but was also slain, as in the case of Paul.[115]

What Farrow's reading (and also O'Donovan's) does not fully adequately expound is the character of the ascension as denoting the time of Christ's ongoing *self*-disclosure. He discloses himself through Word and Spirit via definite courses of action: namely, those that humanize. In so doing, Christ surpasses his rejection. Elect people live as those for whom their rejection – and also the world's – is slain, as those who participate in Christ's commission to be his witnesses. Therefore, they live in solidarity with others, those who have not become reconciled to what they are, precisely because they recognize that the rejection of those others, too, is surpassed. The moral significance of truth lies in its recognition that rejection – the world's rejection – is radically circumscribed. And so, the gathered community works to articulate moral and social policy that is commensurate with the way things are. It does not consign the world to fate and so works as a community that helps all peoples to see that life does not have to be a certain way. The gathered community does not believe for a moment in 'an ontology-free space', and so helps the mandates given to us – such as work, family, government and church – to be transparent to the real world, to what is coming to pass.

The prophetic office of Christ, as Barth and the Reformed Orthodox describe it, is about far more than the spreading of knowledge of Christ as the high priest and king. It is not solely epistemological in nature, inasmuch as the spreading of knowledge is a spreading that does take us up. Truth in short is profoundly self-involving. It is not a matter of 'like it or lump it' but of promise, of participating in the promise: 'You will be my people' and so become those who listen 'to my voice' (John 18.37). In gathering up a people in whom Judas and Paul live asymmetrically, the truth upholds and accordingly sends us out by virtue of our inclusion in the apostolate to participate by faith in his heavenly session. Indeed, we participate as those called to testify to his ongoing mediatorial work as One who does not will to be himself without his people and thus his Father's world.

---

[115] *CD* II/2, 506.

Chapter 4

ON THE PRESENCE OF CHRIST'S LOVE

To be Jesus Christ is to be present. Jesus' presence is, as I have been arguing all along, but a function of his identity. His identity as One who is present has profound implications for ethics. Ethics, inclusive as it is of the details of moral life, is subject to a going on, to One who is present, and as such active. Specifically, he is present and active as One who gathers, upholds and sends a people forth. It is this third piece, his presence as the One who sends, that shall be my focus for the present chapter. Indeed, I will focus on the resurrected One as One who sends Peter forth and us in him. I will do so in conversation with John 21, the textual witness which establishes Christ as One who sends us forth to feed his sheep in his name. Indeed, He is the One whom we follow, the One who is always ahead of us, rendering us through his Word and Spirit participant in where he is and in what he is doing: namely, caring for and tending his sheep.

In reading the Scriptures, the point I hope, first and foremost, to make is a simple one, namely that Scripture construes ethical reality. It shows us the goings on that characterize the real world. Scripture lives, inasmuch as its subject matter lives. He lives, and so do these texts as a result. They are the appointed place where he speaks himself and the command that is ingredient in his self-attestation: 'Follow me'. Therefore, it is imperative that we attend to the text of John 21 as bespeaking an event that is 'most up-to-date', and to inquire after what manner of participation these texts generate in response to the contemporary event that lies at their heart.[1] Second, John 21, as with John 5 and the trial scenes, identifies a particular agent who is, as the eternal One, our contemporary. The second section of the chapter will be a hearing of the ways in which the

---

[1] *CD* IV/2, 107.

history of this One is, precisely in its 'then-ness' also 'here and now'. Specifically, I hear John 21 as announcing a person who in all of his historical particularity is, as the risen and ascended One, *now*. But that this One who is now as he was then, that he can be this One, is precisely a function of his always being the eternal Son of the Father together with the Holy Spirit. That is, it is his eternal identity as the Son of God that is the basis for his showing or his manifesting himself then and so now. Third, I will ask after the way in which this One who is reality, whose identity is disclosive of reality and establishes reality, is also command. That is to say, the Christ whose love is present, commands us to love as he does. However, his love is not present in like manner to a thud. Rather, through his Word and Spirit he gives and imparts what he commands. The power to 'do likewise', to affirmatively answer the question posed to Peter 'Do you love me?', he grants by his Spirit. Fourth and last, I shall reflect on the moral significance and entailments of the presence of such love. Although my intention in this section is not to answer the 'What shall we do question?' in exhaustive fashion, I suggest that the way in which we answer that question is radically dependent on what *is* being done.[2] The question of the presence of One whose person evokes a radical doing has all the import in the world for the details of moral life. In short, we are to love one another, in a manner transparent to the presence of that Other, he whose love is in-breaking in a way that accords with his ascended and glorified humanity.

THE WITNESS TO LOVE: JOHN 21

John 21, which records Jesus' appearance to the seven disciples, to Peter, and to the Beloved Disciple, is the last recorded manifestation of Jesus in John's Gospel. In Hoskyns's words, 'The scene is one of complete apostasy, and is the fulfilment of xvi.32.'[3] The disciples have scattered with every intention of leaving the Lord behind: hence their going fishing. They return to what they did prior to Jesus' encounter of them. The fact that Jesus appears, that he 'showed (*ephanerōsen*) himself in this way', and that it is the 'disciple whom Jesus loved (*ēgapa*)' who perceives that it is the Lord and tells Peter

---

[2] So Morse: 'The Gospel's proclamation of Jesus' kingdom as not *from* this world but as coming to this world is parabolically signified and apocalyptically realized as heavenly life taking place now at hand.' *The Difference Heaven Makes*, 108.

[3] Hoskyns, *Fourth Gospel*, 2:660.

is significant (John 21.1, 7). The verb *phaneroun*, which is used nine times in the Gospel, occurs twice in 21.1. Raymond Brown comments, 'It has the general connotation of emergence from obscurity, and for John involves a concrete revelation of the heavenly upon earth.'[4] Accordingly, Jesus wills to manifest himself once more as the One he is before his faithless followers.

What the beloved disciple recognizes, precisely because, as will be later explained via Augustine, he loves Christ the more, is precisely what is going on. The beloved disciple perceives in a manner unlike the others just who it is who is present on the shore. Perception of the One who is present and who speaks is possible to the extent that the 'future life of ours that is yet to come', that life when we shall see 'face to face', impinges upon us, enabling us to see the one who is there calling to us.[5] Accordingly, the beloved disciple sees. The beloved disciple is, in a sense, the counterpart to Peter (and the rest) who cannot perceive the One present and calling. It is after all he who, as John describes in 20.8, reaches the tomb first and 'saw and believed' (John 20.8). The same is not said of Peter. He, like the rest, is apostate.

The One who calls from the shore enables a miraculous catch of fish. Hitherto his showing himself, the nets remained empty; the disciples' labor is without purpose. 'Alone they can neither catch fish, nor bring them to land, even if they do catch them: *Apart from me ye can do nothing*.'[6] However, the miraculous haul of fish, and the meal by the shore, chastens the apostasy of the disciples. 'Now none of the disciples dared to ask him, "Who are you?" because they knew it was the Lord' (John 21.3). The Lord appeared to them in a way which required no explanation, as is the case with Peter's great haul of fishes as recorded in Luke 5.4-11. In Luke 5.4-11 the recognition that it is the Lord who calls, and Peter's recognition of his sinfulness in the presence of divinity, only follows upon the miraculous haul of fish. But in John 21.15-23, which has as its theme the sending and future of Peter, Peter does not tell the Lord to go away. Instead, he confesses love for him. Luke 5.4-11 is an anticipation of Easter. In John 21.1-14,

---

[4] Raymond E. Brown, *The Gospel According to John: XIII–XXI* (2 vols; Anchor Bible, 29–29A; Garden City, NY: Doubleday, 1970), 2:1067.

[5] Philip Schaff (ed.), *The Nicene and Post-Nicene Fathers of the Christian Church*, 1st series, vol. 7, *St. Augustin: Homilies on the Gospel of John; Homilies on the First Epistle of John; Soliloquies* (1886–1889; repr., Edinburgh: T&T Clark,1986), 124.6 (hereafter cited as *NPNF* 7); and 1 Cor. 13.12.

[6] Hoskyns, *Fourth Gospel*, 2:663, original emphasis; and John 15.5.

Easter is not anticipated but actualized in the Lord's reign of life signified by the abundance of fishes.

The One who is Easter – the resurrection and life – appears to the seven disciples, calling them, but in a way in which the call given to them is One that proceeds through Peter and is in a sense exemplified by the beloved. Indeed, the seven are commissioned through the commission explicitly given to Peter. Peter (and the rest) will indeed 'be catching people' (Luke 5.10). But they will be doing so in a way that accords with their being commanded through Peter to 'Feed (also tend) my sheep'. The duty of an apostle is not only to catch but also to care for those whom the Gospel proclamation catches. It is to shepherd the sheep in the presence of the Shepherd. This Peter can now do. Peter's threefold confession of love, which of course parallels his threefold denial, is precisely what will enable him to 'steadfastly persevere in this office', the office being that of feeding and tending the sheep.[7] His confession of love is, for Calvin, to so reign 'in his heart that forgetting himself and devoting himself entirely to Him, he surmounts every obstacle... Those called to govern the Church should therefore remember that if they want to discharge their office truly and properly, they must start off from the love of Christ.'[8] It is Jesus' love for Peter that is being done into Peter himself, so that Peter can in return feed those others whom Christ loves.

What is so very instructive about Calvin's exegesis is that the task which Peter (and the rest of the apostolate and us in them) is given is that of loving Christ. Peter cannot carry on with his apostolic appointment, calling and commission without his heart being filled with 'unshakable love' for the Lord.[9] Only such love will be able to sustain him in 'the complete *imitatio Christi*...[as] both Shepherd and Martyr'.[10] Love for the One, who shows himself and in showing himself commissions, requires the love of the Shepherd which discloses itself in care for the Shepherd's sheep.

That Jesus 'showed himself in this way' as the One who commissions is, if Calvin's and Hoskyns's readings are correct, said also to 'those called to govern the church'.[11] Jesus' appearance and, more specifically, dialogue with Peter assumes a universal horizon. Says

---

[7] Calvin, *Commentary on John 11–21*, 2:219.
[8] Calvin, *Commentary on John 11–21*, 2:219.
[9] Hoskyns, *Fourth Gospel*, 2:665.
[10] Hoskyns, *Fourth Gospel*, 2:665.
[11] Calvin, *Commentary on John 11–21*, 2:219.

Hoskyns: 'The Lord, in the person of Peter, requires of His disciples nothing but love, and recommends to them nothing but the care of His Sheep.'[12] The Lord's words to Peter are words that include the Lord's disciples, that is, not only the remaining six but us in them. The love for the Lord and devotion to the sheep demanded of Peter is demanded of them, too. Peter's faithful discharge of his office is predicated upon 'the love of Christ'. The same is true with respect to his fellow disciples then and there and disciples in the here and now. This is their and our service to Christ. Again, Calvin: 'Nothing more efficacious could have been said for encouraging ministers of the Gospel, than when they hear that the service most agreeable to Christ is that which is expended on feeding His flock.'[13] Peter and us in him are commissioned so as to participate in the ministry of feeding.

Peter and John (The Loved and the Beloved)

Augustine's exegesis of John 21 warrants our attention. For Augustine, this text, which is indicative of there being 'a great mystery in the Gospel of John', is about the engendering of love for Christ. It is, for Augustine, a matter of being present to the Christ who seeks Peter (and us in him) out, in order that those entrusted with the task of feeding Christ's flock might know that they feed those who are his: 'my sheep'. But how to feed best those sheep who are Christ's is Augustine's concern. In order to take up this concern, Augustine offers a sophisticated and dense contrast of Peter and the 'disciple whom Jesus loved' (John 21.20). Peter represents, for Augustine, the Church. The words spoken to Peter – 'Follow me' – assume a universal horizon. 'But to the universality [of the Church] it is said, "Follow me", even as it was for the same universality that Christ suffered.'[14] Peter represents the church, and Christ is understood to be the rock (*petra*). To follow is, simply, to *love* the One whom one follows.

Love of Christ is not something enjoined upon Peter in abstraction from the church. Christ loves Peter and in him the church to the end 'that He may heal and translate us from everything He loveth not'.[15] Christ's love has direction, then: it has teleological force; for it is love that sanctifies. More precisely, it is the Spirit of Christ who is the

[12] Hoskyns, *Fourth Gospel*, 2:666.
[13] Calvin, *Commentary on John 11–21*, 2:219.
[14] *NPNF 7, Augustin: Homilies*, 124, 5.
[15] *NPNF 7, Augustin: Homilies*, 124, 5.

Spirit of his Father, the Holy Spirit, who delivers his people from that whereby they would perish. 'Let Peter therefore love Him, that we may obtain deliverance from our present mortality; let John be loved by Him, that we may be preserved in the immortality to come.'[16] To Peter, and thus to the church, is given a task: to love him who loves us. In so loving him who is present to us, who manifests, shows, appears, and reveals himself to us, we are delivered from our present mortality, that is from the flesh, from that which is antithetical to life.[17]

In Augustine's reading the beloved disciple represents a rather more realized form of discipleship. To John it is not asked: 'Do you love me?' Rather, John is loved by Jesus. Christians are included in John's identity too, as he represents, for Augustine, one who is loved by Christ to the end that 'we may be preserved in the immortality to come'.[18] To Christians is posed the question to Peter: 'Do you love me?' But Christians are also represented by the beloved disciple: the One who questions Christians in Peter is the One in whom we are beloved. Peter, for Augustine, represents the old self, the self who is passing away. John, on the other hand, represents the new self, the self coming to be. The risen Christ who speaks to Peter loves John the more because John symbolizes one whom he loves in 'blessedness'. 'For if Christ loveth us more in the world to come, where we shall live unendingly with Him, than in the present, from which we are in the course of being rescued, that we may be always in the other, it does not follow on that account that we shall love Him less when better ourselves.'[19] John is indeed symbolic of our new form. He is the one to whom Peter (and we in him) aspire, the representative of the world to come in the here and now. John denotes our true self, our better self 'since we can in no possible way be better ourselves, save by loving Him more'.[20]

Augustine's exegesis is particularly instructive, I think, because he perceives how the two disciples represent, respectively, our old and new self. John bespeaks our better self, our true self, one who is

---

[16] *NPNF* 7, *Augustin: Homilies*, 124, 5.

[17] Life (*zōē*) occurs thirty-six times in the Gospel. C. H. Dodd, for example, makes much of the Hebrew antecedents of life eternal in John's Gospel. 'The Hebrew conception of life is always one of action, movement and enjoyment', life which, for John, begins here and now. See *The Interpretation of the Fourth Gospel* (Cambridge: Cambridge University Press, 1970), 150.

[18] *NPNF* 7, *Augustin: Homilies*, 122, 5.

[19] *NPNF* 7, *Augustin: Homilies*, 122, 6.

[20] *NPNF* 7, *Augustin: Homilies*, 122, 6.

more transparent to the love which circumscribes us. Ethics, if I may introduce language not present in John's narrative or in Augustine's and Calvin's commentary, ought not to be chaste about deploying language like love, specifically the ethical import of loving Christ. Ethics is about formation in accord with 'that future life of ours, such as He knows it will be hereafter in us, in order that by so loving us He may draw us onward to its possession'.[21] If ethics is a function, a moment in the love of Christ, it is a moment that is generated by a love that precedes and gives of itself to be loved in the present. The Lord loves in us what is in accord with eternal life, the new creation. Eternal life is for John's Gospel a presently apprehended reality.[22] Our drawing toward that life which is ours is possible, again, because Christ loves us. The order here matters. Peter (and us in him) cannot draw onward to the possession of the life that is to come apart from Christ. The blessedness that is symbolized by the beloved disciple, the fact that this disciple 'loveth the more', is, for Augustine, not because of resources internal to this particular disciple, but rather because the love which confronts Peter is more present in the beloved disciple and so 'maketh him blessed'.[23] The agency is Christ's. It is 'the Lord [who] has Himself diffused this very gospel through the whole world, that every one of His own may drink thereat according to his own individual capacity'.[24] The Lord diffuses the Gospel that makes better, that draws us onwards, that announces: 'Follow me'. The Lord is the active agent in the diffusion of his Gospel that appoints, calls and commissions both Peter and the beloved disciple (and us too, prospectively). The Lord's love is present to them, inclusive of them. It speaks to them, makes them new. But it does not speak the same words. Peter is representative of the apostolate (and of us in them), and so our joy is to follow him in all of the brightness of his works.

A LOVING PRESENCE: ETERNAL AND CONTEMPORARY

John 21.15-20 is something of a description of Peter's return home. Jesus, risen from the dead, having gone into the far country that is death, a death preceded by Peter's threefold denial, is about to return home, to ascend. But he does not will to return home without Peter

[21] *NPNF* 7, *Augustin: Homilies*, 122, 6.
[22] Moody Smith, *Gospel of John*, 59.
[23] *NPNF* 7, *Augustin: Homilies*, 122, 6.
[24] *NPNF* 7, *Augustin: Homilies*, 122, 7.

(and the other apostles and us in them). That Peter returns home, in a manner of speaking, with the threefold declaration 'You know that I love you', is the fruit that Jesus' resurrection bears. Peter (and us as those addressed in his person) has been placed on a higher level, exalted in the One who confronts him with the commission to live a life of following that will be consummated by martyrdom. Taking our cues from Barth, there is in Jesus Christ 'this movement from below to above as it takes place in Him, as His exaltation – the exaltation of man as it has taken place and still takes place in Him'.[25] Peter participates in this exaltation, to be sure; but his exaltation as freedom to participate in his new being, to correspond to it, will take the form of a death wherein he does not wish to go. And yet, his exaltation still stands. It is from this point, in dialogue with Barth, that we can begin to explore the eternal surety of Christ's narratival presence as love which confronts Peter and claims him for the feeding of the sheep and therefore a following unto death. Moreover, we can account for the exaltation to service of the flock as an exaltation that takes place *now*. Christ is at work raising up women and men so as to participate in his ministry of feeding.

The love of Christ places us on a higher level. In him humanity is given to share in his new humanity which is radically distinct from ours – 'not only quantitatively but qualitatively'.[26] In such distinctness, it is also radically alike.[27] That Peter (and us in him) is confronted by One so like us and also so different, One who submitted to his cross and was raised anew as the resurrected and exalted One, is a function of 'God's eternal election of grace [which] is concretely the election of Jesus Christ'.[28] The language of eternal election, of decree, matters a great deal in our case. That the One present on the beach to the seven disciples can indeed show himself as he does is because of the election of grace, that is, 'the decision and action in which God in his Son elected and determined Himself for man, and...man for Himself'.[29] The One whom the beloved perceives to be the Lord is God's decision not only for Peter and the remaining six, but also for all those who obey the Lord via their testimony. Jesus' identity is as the elect One, One whose presence is a function of his

---

[25] *CD* IV/2, 29.
[26] *CD* IV/2, 28.
[27] *CD* IV/2, 28.
[28] *CD* IV/2, 31.
[29] *CD* IV/2, 31.

identity as the One in whom God eternally determines himself to be for humanity and humanity for himself.

The One whom the narrative of John 21 identifies as the Lord is eternal. The election of Jesus Christ is not something that God decides at some point in time but rather that which is in accord with the deepest grain of the universe. Jesus' confrontation with Peter is the second moment of God's eternal election of grace. In his Son God determined himself for humanity and humanity (in this case, Peter) for himself. Peter is confronted with a determination in the form of a question, posed by One who is eternal: 'Do you love me?' Peter is determined by his Lord to be for his Lord. Although Peter denied him thrice, the call and commission to 'follow' is utterly effective, because it bespeaks the 'anthropological side' or 'consequence' of a determination that is immanent and eternal. The covenant is indeed of grace. Its Lord keeps the covenant from his side even unto death.

He who descends, humbles himself even unto death, does so 'in order to lift him [humanity] up so high'.[30] This is Jesus Christ, he who is by nature God with the Father and the Spirit. Human essence is taken by him together with his Father and the Spirit, and so united to his divine nature. The Lord's showing of himself to Peter and the others is a function of his being 'by nature God'. Even death, even the absolute apostasy of his disciples, cannot prevent the Lord from manifesting himself, the eternal Son who is co-equal with the Father and the Spirit.

Thus an account of ethics in the presence of the risen Christ, specifically of Christ's love, that relegates or isolates talk about the Son's ontological self-sufficiency together with the Father and Spirit does so to its detriment. Inasmuch as the Son shows himself this way, he is attesting himself to be the eternal Son who, in Jesus, gives himself to all people, in the case of the narrative Peter. Peter's declaration of fidelity to Jesus is his personal participation, to use explicitly dogmatic language, in the Son of God's determination to unite human essence to his divine essence in the man Jesus. The assumption of flesh by the Son includes the assumption of all people. The Son, who assumes human essence to himself, gives it a share in his divine essence. He cannot be conceived of apart from this determination: it is of an eternal character.

The acting subject of the narrative, 'God Himself in His mode of existence as the Son, who is of one divine essence with the Father

---

[30] *CD* IV/2, 43.

and the Holy Spirit', gives to Peter what is his true end as the man
Peter. Peter in being called to follow (even unto death) is being
called to genuine humanity. 'It is genuinely human in the deepest
sense to live by the electing grace of God addressed to man.'[31] This
grace is addressed to him in the form of a command or commission
issued by One who is the electing grace of God. Peter (and us in
him) is being summoned to be present to and to follow One in whom
human essence is exalted, an exaltation whose subject is the divine
Son become Son of Man who gives to human essence a share in his
divinity. His divinity does not abolish humanity but rather renders it
genuinely humane.

The One who requires love of himself from Peter is precisely
the One who engenders that love. It is to the love that Jesus is, that
Peter is to be present. That Jesus is indeed present to Peter and to
the others (and to us in them) is possible, precisely because Jesus,
although soon to ascend, will yet come to them in the Spirit: 'I am
coming to you' (John 14.18). The Spirit is, to invoke Moody Smith's
words once again, the One who is 'the virtual continuation of his
[Jesus'] own ministry'.[32] Here we see again that the identity of this
One is indissolubly bound up with the Spirit whom he breathes and
sends. 'For He Himself is in heaven with the Father. Here He is for
us and the world in the work of the Holy Spirit.'[33] The eternal and
contemporary identity of Christ can never be divorced from the
Spirit. Identity language is helpful precisely, once again, because
the One who ascended to heaven and is present in the Spirit is in
his very person an event, not a state. The acting subject of Jesus'
humanity, of the hypostatic union, is the divine Son. In him is the
exaltation of human essence, in particular of Peter's 'essence', to love
of himself and the feeding of his sheep. That is an event inasmuch as
the divine Son, who wills it to be, is always the One who achieves it.
State language is far too staid, not nearly dynamic enough, when it
comes to describing the identity of the One who breathes the Spirit,
and in breathing the Spirit can be said to come to his disciples even
as he ascends.

What we are beholding in John 21 and in John 20.19-23 is the
self-positing of the eternal Son, begotten of the Father together with
the Holy Spirit. The Spirit whom the Son breathes is the Spirit He

---

[31] *CD* IV/2, 89.
[32] Moody Smith, *Gospel of John*, 59.
[33] *CD* IV/2, 97.

eternally receives as begotten of the Father. What takes place on 'the first day of the week' and 'by the Sea of Tiberias', to use the language of Barth's theology, is an outworking of the 'execution of the eternal will and decree in which God elected man for Himself and Himself for man, giving even now this concrete determination [*Bestimmung*] to His own divine being'.[34] God in the person of his Son eternally elects, to focus on the second half of Barth's formulation, himself for humankind. And so, what we see taking place is the action of God who, in the person of his Son and with the Spirit whom he breathes, effectively presents himself as the One he eternally is in a manner befitting his human nature. The ground of his action throughout John's narrative, to say nothing of its concluding portion, is his eternal being as the Son of the Father. What he accomplishes in the heart of Peter is, albeit provisionally although nonetheless genuinely, the love he is *in se* together with Father and Spirit. Peter and the other six behold the effective presence of Christ himself, effective in that he does not appear or show himself in his resurrected life to be without the Spirit, the guarantor of the brightness of his works, the very possibility of love of himself.

This is where we can begin, I think, to grapple with his identity as One who is 'the most up-to-date'.[35] His history is indeed 'most up-to-date' because it is a history which possesses a revelatory character. 'For them [the disciples] the Holy Spirit was simply and directly the existence of Jesus Christ as the divine act of majesty in its character as revelation.'[36] Jesus' history is never without the Spirit, the Spirit who accomplishes and is the power of his self-witness. His being as the eternal Son is a revelatory being and thus contemporary, because he is eternally One who receives from the Father the Spirit whom he breathes. In his resurrection 'He reveals Himself as the One who was and is and will be this in His life and death'.[37] He, in other words, is the active agent of his own self-disclosure. That his self-revelation

---

[34] *CD* IV/2, 114 [translation altered]. Note that this is not the place to enter into a discussion of the relationship between election and trinity, as is being debated by the likes of Paul Molnar and Bruce McCormack. My judgments regarding the matter are expressed in '"A Specific Form of Relationship": On the Dogmatic Implications of Barth's Account of Election and Commandment for his Theological Ethics', in *Trinity and Election in Contemporary Theology*, ed. Michael Dempsey (Grand Rapids, MI: Eerdmans, 2011): 188–200.

[35] *CD* IV/2, 107.

[36] *CD* IV/2, 129.

[37] *CD* IV/2, 145.

is effective is because it is never without the Spirit whom he receives and breathes.

In the case of Peter and all those who believe in his Lord through the proclamation of the message, 'a genuine and fruitful knowledge…the knowledge of love for the One who has first loved us in Jesus Christ' arises.[38] 'Genuine and fruitful' knowledge is participatory knowledge, participation in the form of obedience to the commission: 'Follow me' (John 21.19). 'Fruitful' knowledge of Christ is precisely knowledge that recognizes him to be contemporary, to be one whose 'history takes place to-day in the same way as did that yesterday – indeed, as the same history'.[39] He is as One whose history is contemporary because 'He overcomes the barrier of His own time and therefore historical distance'.[40] That he can and does do so is because his being, the being of the man Jesus, is that of the eternal Son who, in uniting human essence to himself in the man Jesus, shows himself to exist humanly in a manner that overcomes historical distance. His being is eternal and as eternal is revelatory and bright. He shines now, because he shone and so will necessarily shine. His history is radiant. It relativizes Lessing's ditch and, in so doing, renders us participant in its forthcoming.

What is declared by John's Gospel in the resurrected Christ's appearance to the disciples, to the seven disciples, and in his harsh exchange with Peter, is what is actual. What is actual is that we are in him and through the Spirit whom he breathes 'concretely seized'.[41] Discipleship is really a matter of being present to this seizure. To be fed is to be seized. The ascended Jesus gathers, upholds, and sends women and men forth through his Word and Spirit so as to participate in his ministry of concretely seizing. The disciples, Jesus will have us believe, are included in Jesus' obedience. This is what marks them off from the world. Through their obedience, but not in a way that is either imprisoned by it or the lack thereof, Jesus through the Spirit continues his ministry of fishing for people.

The Son of God's self-presentation as the One who fulfills the covenant and reconstitutes his people Israel around himself is of the character of reality. He, as a function of his always being the Son begotten of the Father together with the Holy Spirit, is ultimate reality.

---

[38] *CD* IV/2, 149.
[39] *CD* IV/2, 107.
[40] *CD* IV/2, 112.
[41] *CD* IV/2, 303.

As such, he is past and present and future. He is, more specifically, a past and present movement, the One who through his cross reconciled the world to himself and through the Spirit whom he breathes draws women and men into the realm of his reconciliation. Peter (and we in him) do not seek Christ. The disciples go fishing; they are apostate. Their action bespeaks the universal human condition. And yet, Jesus 'showed himself in this way' (John 21.1). He shows himself in a way that makes Peter Christian and into a Christian. In Jesus' presence Peter becomes what he is. 'In Jesus Christ a Christian has already come into being, but in himself and his time he is always in the process of becoming.'[42] What will happen in Peter's life, his being taken where he would 'not wish to go', is a matter of him being borne by One who wills him to become what he is in him, to 'follow him'.

The disciples by returning to fishing demonstrate their failure to recognize that they are caught up in a real movement. 'It belongs to the real concept of the worldly that it is at all times seen in the movement of the world's both having been accepted and becoming accepted by God in Christ.'[43] The beloved disciple is accepted, Peter is becoming accepted. The beloved disciple leads a life of harmony with the will of God. The life to which we are passing is his. And that life that is truly life, the resurrection and the life, 'is power aimed at the establishment of genuine human life'.[44] This life is being realized in Peter; in a sense, it has already been realized in the beloved. It is Peter who is to follow the Christ who will soon ascend '"to my Father and your Father, to my God and your God"' (John 20.17). In following, he will continually receive Jesus Christ through the Spirit. By the Spirit in whom the ascended Jesus comes, 'we enter into the sphere of His presence and action and lordship'.[45] It is to this sphere that Peter is summoned, a summons in the Spirit that will eventually take the form of martyrdom. The anthropological correlate in Peter's case is that Christ's presence to him in the Spirit commissions him to be present to Christ even unto his own death.

The power of the resurrected One is 'power that aims at human life'.[46] The risen Lord is effectively present to human life because to be himself is just to be One who reveals himself. His being is

---

[42] *CD* IV/2, 307.
[43] *DBW*, vol. 6, *Ethics*, 59.
[44] *CD* IV/2, 316.
[45] *CD* IV/2, 323.
[46] *CD* IV/2, 316.

revelatory; it shines and so humanizes human life in accordance with the light it always is. This is why we must talk about him in a manner appropriate to the narrative that narrates him. That he shows himself, and does so effectively in the Spirit, is because his being is eternally luminous. His being sent by the Father and his ascending to the Father with us along with him are, by the Spirit's power, two different moments in which he shines as the One he is. We cannot know the history of this One without being implicated by it, because to know him is to know ourselves *in* him, in the event of his existence.

His existence is a fruitful one in that it gives rise to those who follow. That it does so is God's work, the work of the Spirit. Barth refers to this as the 'goal' of the existence of the crucified, risen and ascended Jesus. His existence is inclusive of a goal: the Christian community and individual Christians. The goal is no less God's work than the basis. The confrontation with Peter, the transformation of Peter into a lover of Christ, a tender of the sheep, a follower, is the work of the Spirit as the 'living transition' from Christ to Christendom. This is an amplification of the point made earlier. The Gospels do not give us a naked Christ. Christ Jesus as narratively attested is One whose identity can never be said to be fully expounded without his appointment, calling and commissioning of the Twelve and of his gathering, upholding and sending of us in them.[47]

He *is* as One who breathes the Spirit who sends them, and us in them, forth. Christ and Christians – and in that order, to be sure – is another way of saying Jesus and the Spirit, the Spirit by whose power the distance between the one man and the many who follow him is overcome. This is the theological basis of a description of the eternal Son as our contemporary. The Son as the revelation of the Father, the revealer, breathes the Spirit who mediates between Christ and Christendom as 'the mode of being of the one God which unites the Father and the Son'.[48] As the One who unites, the Spirit draws human beings to the Son who has united human essence to himself in the man Jesus Christ. Peter, the disciples and we as those who hear and obey their message are participants in the triune life, the life that repeats itself in our history. 'God Himself lives' in the transition between Christ and Peter, God being the Spirit. And 'God Himself lives' in the transition between the Christ and we who believe in him through his self-testimony via the apostolic

[47] See Demson, *Barth and Frei*, 48.
[48] *CD* IV/2, 339.

testimony.[49] Peter, no less than ourselves, beholds the Trinity doing its thing, bringing humanity along for the ride, as the triune God expresses himself in this his history.

Note, however, that there is a moment of reserve – or better, 'anticipation' – in all this. Barth writes, 'in anticipation His existence includes within itself our existence with Him'.[50] That is to say, we are becoming Christians; we but follow. Of course our existence is in him in an objective sense; yet what is objective presses for subjective realization. The Son of the Father is present by the Spirit whom he breathes. All of the use of event language in describing Christ as One both eternal and contemporary, One who is present as the love he elicits in the Spirit, functions to safeguard the basic truth that the Godhead is not static. The covenant of grace as the dynamic reiteration of God's triune life is generative of covenant partners, men and women who participate in the free occurrence of the triune life. The basis of the partnership is always God's triune life, 'the living act which He directs towards us'.[51]

It is the Spirit, moreover, who unites us to the Son of the Father who wills to be glorified by our action in the following of his Son. Far from overlaying a speculative metaphysics on John 21, the passage demands such reflection as an identity is narrated which is never abstracted from the Spirit whom he breathes, whose history is the reflection and correspondence of the eternal event in which God is Father, Son and Holy Spirit. God himself is present in the Spirit who enables us to live with and follow God himself. Jesus ascends. But he ascends only to come, and is present in the manner of anticipation, in order to feed through his disciples the world he came to save in order that it too might live and be present to himself. 'We can cling to the fact that by the Holy Spirit we may be and live with God Himself… But we may do so without reserve, because in His Spirit God Himself is present.'[52]

THE COMMAND TO LOVE: FOLLOW ME

The task in this penultimate section is to ask after the sense in which Christ can be said to be One who is present in the form of command,

---

[49] *CD* IV/2, 342.
[50] *CD* IV/2, 342.
[51] *CD* IV/2, 345.
[52] *CD* IV/2, 347.

specifically the command to love. In John 21 Christ gives himself to Peter in the form of a commission: 'Feed my sheep' and a command 'Follow me'. Christ is present to Peter in the imperative: 'You will stretch out your hands, and someone else will fasten a belt around you and take you where you do not wish to go' (John 21.18). Peter is told the truth about himself: he is to be a martyr. Moreover, Peter is confronted by One who is present to him in the form of a command: 'Follow me'. The imperative follows the indicative. As one loved, Peter is called to die for his Lord.

Bonhoeffer is especially helpful in enabling us to understand better the relationship between the indicative and the imperative, a relationship crucial for establishing the dogmatic foundation of ethics. He avers that the relationship between the 'ought and is... between past and present,... [is] the relationship between Jesus Christ and the Holy Spirit'.[53] Indeed, this is crucial to recognize, for if the second section of the chapter is description of the 'is', the eternal and contemporary presence of One who *is* love, then the third section is a conceptual expansion of the 'ought' as included in the 'is'. It is to describe the command that such present love is in explicitly pneumatological terms. Stated somewhat differently, I am continuing to argue that Christology is the key to ethics, a move that necessarily leads in the direction of pneumatological territory. There is not in Jesus Christ any antipathy between the 'ought' and the 'is'. They are united in him. That is to say, Jesus is never in the New Testament described as being without the Spirit whom he receives and sends, whom he breathes, the very power of his self-witness.

When I argue that Christ is present in the form of command, I mean to say that he is present *in* the Spirit. In participating in Christ, we participate in his being filled with the Spirit whom he receives from the Father and sends. The presence of Christ contains direction, what St. Paul calls the 'law (*nomos*) of the Spirit of life' (Rom. 8.2). This is the law to which we, as those before him, are to submit. In the words of the early Bonhoeffer,

> Only when we acknowledge that the decision has already taken place, the beginning has already been made, the deed already done, and done by God; only when we are met by the decision, the beginning, God's deed, and know that we are drawn into it can we hear the commandment of God as the law of life for those for whom God long since has done everything and who now are 'in the law'.[54]

[53] *DBW*, vol. 6, *Ethics*, 50.
[54] Dietrich Bonhoeffer, *Meditating on the Word*, ed. and trans. David McI. Gracie (Cambridge, MA: Cowley, 1986), 108.

The One present to us is indeed present in the form of the law, as command, as a 'Do this'. But he is present as this One in the power of the Spirit – and that makes all the difference because his burden and yoke thus become 'light'.

Indeed, what is 'extraordinary' in all of this is that we follow the One whom we are. Paul's dictum – in Christ – is again relevant at just this point. There is One ahead of Peter and thus One ahead of us, One whom we follow. But he is ahead of us in a way which involves his simultaneously coming to us. He is ahead of us even as we are *in* him. The 'I am coming to you' of John 14.18 is important. He comes to us in his Spirit, for the Spirit of the Father 'is his own Spirit'.[55] 'Coming' language is another way of attesting the fact that we cannot escape him; human essence, by virtue of the hypostatic union, is *in* him. The Son possesses, for Cyril of Alexandria, the Spirit 'in the same way as one would conceive of the Father possessing him [the Son], that is, not as something added on, or of external origin'.[56] To be sure, Cyril avers that the Spirit is a different hypostasis than the Son. And yet, the Spirit possesses 'such a close likeness to himself [the Son] and with the power to operate in a manner identical to that in which he himself might perhaps do, that he appears to be the Son himself and not at all different'.[57] Thus when we talk about the command of Christ's love, we are talking about a command that can never be isolated from the Giver of the command, a Giver who although present at the right hand of his Father, is simultaneously present in the Spirit. The Spirit indeed 'appears to be the Son himself', and so is the power to keep and fulfil what the Son commands.

The command to love, which is to care for and to feed the sheep, is a command which is pneumatologically realized. If what happens to Jesus is that which happens to each and every person, then human beings enjoy a share in the Spirit not as something added on to them, but rather as the third person whom we too are in, inasmuch as we are in the Son. If the Son is present in his ascended mode by the Spirit, then the command to love is the command to be present to the Son through his Word and Spirit who indwells and promises to fill those who call upon him. The 'follow me' is issued by an agent who presents himself in the mode of command, which is simultane-

[55] Cyril, *Commentary on John*, John 14.16-17, 123.
[56] Cyril, *Commentary on John*, 123.
[57] Cyril, *Commentary on John*, 123.

ously the mode of promise: the Spirit is the power to obey what he commands.

The command is ingredient in himself; for the Spirit is part of the self that the Son speaks. Robert Jenson states that 'it is the Spirit who makes the gospel an actual and so potent word, a "word-event", if one will, but the Spirit's efficacy is not simply other than the Son's personal subjectivity as one who identifies *himself* to his people; thus Paul can even say, precisely in this context, "The Lord is the Spirit" '.[58] The command of the Son is actualized in the Spirit as *his* command: 'Follow me'. The command then does not remain something confined to the past, something to be casuistically applied to goings on to which it is fundamentally alien. By no means: the Son is present in the Spirit as command: 'Follow me'. It is as if the Son were to say: 'I am at work; follow me in this work and thus participate in it.' His presence is command, for he is present in the Spirit as a 'Do this' in the form of 'Follow me'. One cannot separate Christ from the Spirit and thus from the command, the law.

The command to follow is the command by which we are kept present to him. This is why it can be said to be a command origi-nating in love. His presence is what creates obedience and indeed illuminates disobedience. This is, I think, what Bonhoeffer is getting at in *Discipleship*, when he argues that 'Discipleship, as allegiance to the person of Jesus Christ, places the follower under the law of Christ, that is, under the cross.'[59] To be under the cross is to be under the Lordship of a person. But this person is risen and ascended and ahead of us in his Spirit as a commanding presence. He indeed comes to us as command: 'Follow me'. Command is the mode of his presence, the way in which he binds us to the love he is. If the event that he is still takes place, is most up-to-date, then following him always maintains the character of simply following, not realizing.

COMMAND AS GOSPEL

To be risen, as Christ is, is ingredient in his identity as narrated in the Gospel. He is risen, moreover, as One who is *for* his disciples and us in them. His presence as this person is as a commanding presence. This is precisely the way in which he is present for us – as command.

---

[58] Robert W. Jenson, *Systematic Theology*, vol. 1, *The Triune God* (New York: Oxford University Press, 1997), 173.

[59] *DBW*, vol. 4, *Discipleship*, 85.

His presence implicates. Indeed, God is present in a ubiquitous sense throughout creation insofar as all things are present to him; but he is present, in a concrete and salutary way to faith, in the risen and ascended Christ who presents himself as a loving 'Do this'. Christ is present, as risen, as law or command but never as an ideal. The command to pastor, to love the sheep, is not an ideal that 'man seeks to realize in history', a command that 'he conceives to be already the truest reality – that is, its final essence'.[60] The command that Jesus gives to Peter and to all the disciples (and us in them) is 'Follow me'. This command cannot be realized in history, for it is already present in and to men and women. The One who commands is also the One who follows the will of his Father even unto death. Christ is, to use Niebuhr's language, the 'pure form' of the command.[61] But the command he is and gives is not to be realized by us but rather by himself working through us in the Spirit whom he breathes, to the end that we might be those who love him, who correspond to the love that he is and gives.

Thus ethics – or better, obedience to the command – cannot, following Niebuhr, be reduced to 'canonical moral codes'.[62] But over and against Niebuhr, the will of God is not a transcendent ideal. The presence of the One who is command – 'Follow me' – does not generate 'transcendent ideals of Christian morality'.[63] To be sure, I do concur with Niebuhr that the possibility of correspondence to Christ's command is not an immanent possibility. The kind of Christology I am advocating is one that is radically generative: obedience is ingredient in the new creation. The Christ who is present to Peter, to his disciples, and to us in them in the Spirit as command fulfills what he commands in us through the Spirit whom he breathes. This is not to say that 'we see in a mirror, dimly' (1 Cor. 13.12). Nonetheless, it is unhelpful to talk about the command to love, feed and follow as an ideal abstracted from the One who speaks the command and gives, in turn, the power to obey.

This is why the command to follow is ingredient in the Gospel: it is good news. It is about living transparently not to an ethic of a person, but rather in harmony *with* a person who is present and active in his Spirit as the love he is. Jesus does not give us 'love ethics'.[64] Likewise, it is not his 'religio-moral insight' articulated, for example, in the Sermon on the Mount that matters.[65] What matters, instead, is his identity as one who is present in the form of command. Jesus' person is indeed command. What Niebuhr actually does is to reduce Jesus to a law-giver, to an ethic, the giver no less of a 'pure religious ethic' that does not generate a robustly 'social ethic'.[66] Accordingly, what matters is not so much his person but rather what he demands, which is, it is important to note, 'incapable of fulfilment in the present existence of man'.[67] 'The law of love' is the 'impossible possibility'.[68] What I am arguing, however, is that Jesus does not give us less than himself. This is the force of the promise of the 'I am coming to you', meaning that Jesus does not give us an ethic; his life, his ministry, cannot be reduced to a love ethic (John 13.18). Our hope is not 'the moral qualities of Christ'.[69] Rather, the Christ 'who became for us wisdom from God, and righteousness and sanctification and redemption' is our hope (1 Cor 1.30). But as hope he is not so much generative 'of a type of optimism which places its ultimate confidence in the love of God and not the love of man'.[70] Rather, he is the enactor of a strange new world, the life of which through his Spirit is being done into us: declared and made righteous.

What Niebuhr's account lacks is an operative sense in which Jesus through his Spirit accomplishes what he commands. His love, the love he is and commands, is present, becoming real. He does not leave us with a law – the law of love – which we must approximate and apply to specific situations using our own resources. The language of approximation and application trades upon his absence. But he cannot be absent, for to be the person he is, is to be present in Word and Spirit. The contexts in which we find ourselves are not contexts to which we must summon him, contexts which call forth prophetic insights brought to the fore on the basis of his life. Instead, the command of Christ is utterly dependent for its intelligibility on its

---

[64] Niebuhr, *Christian Ethics*, 49.
[65] Niebuhr, *Christian Ethics*, 58.
[66] Niebuhr, *Christian Ethics*, 61.
[67] Niebuhr, *Christian Ethics*, 67.
[68] Niebuhr, *Christian Ethics*, 69.
[69] Niebuhr, *Christian Ethics*, 131.
[70] Niebuhr, *Christian Ethics*, 131.

environment. Its environment is such that he not only is a pattern of what he commands but cause; he is model and means.[71]

This is why the command to love is good news. Not only is command never abstracted from the One who commands, he is present as commander in his Spirit. 'The Holy Spirit remains instead the motor of all that we become, of both our new dispositions and what follows from them.'[72] A serious Christology is inclusive of a robust pneumatology. 'The mission of the Son is to give us his own Spirit, which conforms us to himself.'[73] This is ultimately what is lacking in Niebuhr, namely the sense in which 'the moral qualities of the Christ' – a phrase which needs serious dogmatic supplication – are brought about by that same Christ thorough his Spirit.[74] This is the Christ whom we follow and imitate. That we can and do indeed follow and imitate is precisely because of himself and his Spirit. He cannot not be present to us without what he 'has achieved... [becoming] ours through him'.[75] This is the miracle of the resurrection narrative in John. The One who presents himself to Peter (and to all his followers) achieves what he commands. Peter will indeed die the death of a martyr out of love for his Lord. This is the promise under which we stand. Ethics in the presence of Christ is ethics in the presence of the promise, the following of One who is coming, who never manifests himself as the resurrected One without the gift of the Spirit.

It is here that we can draw this section to a close. The risen Christ is present in John as an event, a happening, something that is taking place, One who does not take place without engaging the disciples and us in them in what is happening. Herein lies the primary difference between my account and that of Niebuhr's. For Niebuhr, we encounter what ought to happen but never can because of sin. Whereas in the approach I am taking, there is an ought – the command to 'follow'. However, the command is reflective of a state of affairs 'actually happening'.[76] Thus, what God in Christ is now doing is what he did then, and so is now present gathering, upholding, and sending women and men in his name in the power of his Spirit. The present situation is a situation subject to One who is present as

---

[71] See Tanner, *Christ the Key*, 57.

[72] Tanner, *Christ the Key*, 84.

[73] Tanner, *Christ the Key*, 173.

[74] Niebuhr, *Christian Ethics*, 131.

[75] Tanner, *Christ the Key*, 102.

[76] Morse, *Difference Heaven Makes*, 82.

command. The command he is and gives reaches us *in* the Spirit. He enables through himself and through the Spirit whom he breathes, women and men, his followers, to participate in what he calls forth: love of himself. He is coming as One shaping events. 'The generative sense of command that calls *forth* what is called *for* is neither simply an obligation demanded nor a categorical imperative grounded in Kantian assumptions of moral autonomy.'[77] Rather, what renders the command to follow, as issued by One who is coming, as other than 'obligation demanded' or 'categorical imperative', is that he together with his Spirit makes possible what he would have us do. And what is that but to love himself and the neighbor in his name. What is coming to us is a love that refuses to manifest or show itself in a way that generates despair or an other-worldly hope. The command to follow is one of love because the One followed always presents himself to his followers as the love that he is and engenders.

THE MORAL SIGNIFICANCE OF THE PRESENCE OF CHRIST'S LOVE: MISSION AND CATECHESIS

It is the basic thesis of this chapter that the risen and ascended Christ is present in the Spirit as One active and ministering the love he is. To be the One he is, is to be present, and his presence is as One who attests, nay spreads, the love that he is. While it is not the intention of this last section to go into any great detail surrounding the moral entailments of the present spreading of such love, it would be good to reflect for a moment as to why, before I give a brief account of something of the difference the presence of Christ's love makes.

My reason for not going into great detail regarding moral entailments is that I want to concentrate on the implications of Jesus' words to Peter, the 'until I come', for moral life in a way that, while mindful of moral policy particulars, does not get overwhelmed by them.[78] Indeed, I do not want to avoid discussion of the details of moral life because of a false privileging of the negative moment of the Gospel: the abolition of creaturely attempts to live in accord with the grain of the universe. Quite the opposite: my attempt throughout this essay has been to get at the Gospel in a way that does not privilege only

---

[77] Morse, *Difference Heaven Makes*, 95, original emphasis.

[78] John 21.22-23. See further my essay, 'Barth on the Economy: In Dialogue with Kathryn Tanner', in *Commanding Grace: Studies in Karl Barth's Ethics*, ed. Daniel L. Migliore (Grand Rapids, MI: Eerdmans, 2010), 198–215.

the negative: the Gospel of Christ establishes a new world that is not in accord with what is passing away but rather with what is coming to pass and with what shall be. The significance of the 'Until I come' functions as a stark reminder that something is coming to pass until Christ comes again. Accordingly, Christ is not in a kind of inert heavenly state. He is active in a manner appropriate to his ascension at the right hand of the Father as prophet, priest and king.

What is coming to pass must be accounted for in the light of where Christ is. 'Whoever serves me must follow me, and where I am, there will my servant be also' (John 12.26). Where Christ is, following the Ephesian Paul, is at the Father's 'right hand in the heavenly places, far above all rule and authority and power and dominion, and above every name that is named, not only in this age but also in the age to come' (Eph. 1.20-21). This is where we are too as those who are in him. And yet, we are there with him in the mode of promise and of anticipation. As such, his followers are here, and yet they are simultaneously with him in the 'heavenly places'. If it be true that what happens to Jesus happens to us, as Bonhoeffer maintains, is indeed realized in us, we might then say that our being with him in the 'heavenly places' until he comes again has profound moral implications. Just as to be in Christ means to be in his ministry as the recapitulation of the first Adam's sordid history; to be in his death is to be in his crucifixion of that history of rebellion; to be in his resurrection is to be in his Father's vindication of his life and ministry as One filled with his own Spirit and faithful to his will; so to be in his ascension is to be radically present in an anticipatory sense – that is, non-spatially – to him. This is what it means to say that the ascension is realized in women and men.

Living in the presence of Christ's love is a matter of facing the future as one over which he presides and the future as in a sense proleptically here in the mode of his promise. His identity as one raised and coming again is generative of ethics, of human activity that participates in his ministry. This, I think, generates a genuine appreciation of the fact that the Gospel pronounces a No – the no to sin and death; but that the No is encompassed by an ever greater Yes that evokes patterns of life commensurate with itself. Faith in the Yes of God just is a matter of being situated by Another. This person determines the context in which we find ourselves as one that is permeated by and, let us pray, permeable to his love.

The moral significance, if you will, of such love is that it is generative of a life lived before God. That is the function of apocalyptic language, of revelation: life lived in the presence of God in Christ through the Spirit. Ascension and ethics are rarely thought of as being inseparably bound up with one another. And yet, they are. For to be where Christ is, is to be where his servants are. Of course his servants are not where he is in a spatial sense: they are here as those who hear the words spoken to Peter as words which remind us that he is coming, that we live in the light of his advent. The 'living in the light of' means that there is space for ministry, for the mission of the church. This is of course not ministry in the name of an absent Christ but rather ministry in the name of a Christ who is ministering. The church's mission has integrity, then, not as a mission that extends Christ but rather as a ministry that is rooted in 'actualities'.[79] The church's kerygma is declarative of what is actual with respect to other people. What is actual, in greater detail, is that its (the world's) history is *with* Christ. To be sure, the church believes that in Jesus' history its own history has already happened. The news that it heralds to the world is that its history has already happened too, and that this history wills to be done into itself. This is the church's mission: to herald what has taken and is taking place, and so to believe and obey.

This is where we begin to see talk of the moral significance of Christ's love best unfolded. If, as Barth maintains, the church is of the character of a 'missionary community [*Missionsgemeinde*]' as a community gathered, upheld and sent by its Lord, then ethics is closely aligned to mission.[80] Stated differently, ethics – human activity exemplary of life lived *coram Deo* – as that which is established in relation to the present Christ, denotes action which is participant in his mission. Christ's history (which is inclusive of his mission) is the Christian community's 'model and pattern'.[81] His coming again does not signify that his mission is no longer operative. Instead, the risen Christ's affirmation that he is coming again means that his followers are enrolled by the power of the Spirit in the school of the apostles. The Twelve apostles are appointed, called and commissioned; and we Gentiles are those whom Christ continues to gather, uphold and send by our inclusion in his appointment, calling and commissioning of the Twelve.[82] This is crucial to bring to the fore, for Christ is continually present only as One who

---

[79] *CD* IV/2, 275.
[80] *CD* IV/2, 275 [translation altered].
[81] *CD* IV/2, 277.
[82] See Demson, *Barth and Frei*, 48.

gathers, upholds and sends 'many (or all) others by including them in his appointment, calling, and commission of the twelve'.[83] If his presence is a gathering, upholding and sending presence, then we cannot talk about his activity as the ascended One in staid terms. As the ascended One he is active, and his mission in the Spirit is but his inclusion of many or all in his appointment, calling and commission of the Twelve.

This is not to compromise the 'once-for-all' character of his ministry. But it is to emphasize that it continues to take place 'once for all'. In this there lies tremendous moral significance. That we live in the presence of One whose love is such that he continues to do that which led to his crucifixion is hard to fathom. He does not leave his followers, however, to do that which ultimately led to his death. His sacrifice is once and for all. Indeed, his reconstitution of his people Israel around himself continues, inasmuch as he is present as One gathering, upholding and sending Jews and Gentiles forth, in order that the fullness of Israel might come to partake in the blessings of covenantal life. This, we can truly say, *is* an event. Were his ascension to the heavenly places a 'state', he could not be said to be 'present except as the One who indefatigably continues to gather, uphold, and send many (or all) others'.[84] But since in his person – the hypostatic union of divinity and humanity in Jesus Christ – he assumes the 'likeness of sinful flesh' in order to reconcile it to his Father, he is best described as an event which can only be said to take place as a presence taking place.[85] Again: he continues to gather, uphold and send many or all others.

Christ's love is utterly luminous in that he continues now to shine and to do what he did then, and in so doing he gathers a people to participate and share in his work of mission, his healing of the nations. His mission – the revealing of his once-and-for-all reconciliation of all flesh to God – is indeed but the result of his concrete direction. His mission takes up human work subject to the power of his direction. Just as is the case with the character of his presence, his mission and our participation in it cannot be described apart from the person and work of the Holy Spirit. The Spirit is the guarantor of the significance – or better, power – of his presence. Ethics – including mission – is but activity circumscribed by 'the dynamic of the indication given by

[83] See Demson, *Barth and Frei*, 48.
[84] See Demson, *Barth and Frei*, 48.
[85] Rom. 8.3.

the Holy Spirit'.[86] The language of 'dynamic' is crucial to recognize; the Spirit is the person of God who establishes people in the one sure foundation of Christ Jesus. Christ is risen and ascended as One present, present to his followers and world as the love that transforms in the Spirit. The Son directs; that his direction takes a radical, unconditional form that guides and corrects is because of the Spirit. Mission, in this sense, is simply a gloss, then, on the basic truth that Christ is not present except as One who gathers, upholds and sends in the power of the Spirit whom he breathes.

The matter of significance, it seems, is also one of instruction. 'He [the Spirit] is the One – and this is His instruction – who actually reveals and makes known and imparts and writes on our heart and conscience the will of God as it applies to us concretely here and now, the command of God in the individual and specific form in which we have to respect it in our own situation.'[87] The will of God is present to his people, and concretely so, *in* the Holy Spirit. This is why we cannot talk about Christ in only the indicative sense. He too is an imperative, and he is this in the Holy Spirit. To live in the presence of his love is to live by his Spirit. Accordingly, our situation is not impermeable to his direction. His direction has power in the Spirit. The Son's presence is thus a powerfully directive One, and never coercive, because He is present through the Spirit in the form of instruction that is as 'a concrete assignment'.[88]

The details of the moral life do matter a great deal. However, one cannot get at the details that really do matter a great deal apart from calling upon the Spirit, the very power of the Son's instruction. Indeed, the instruction of the Son in the Spirit is terribly precise, and so therefore cannot 'be caught up by man into any general law, or subjected to any regulation, or pin-pointed in a written code. Surely this is quite impossible when the Holy Spirit is Himself our law and rule…, and when His instruction is the commanding of the living God which has to be heard directly and continuously by the community and the individual Christian'.[89] What Barth is arguing for is not a privileging of the negative moment in the moral life – that of disruption. Rather, he is averring that the details of the moral life do matter, but only when we recognize that the law and rule of

---

[86] *CD* IV/2, 366.
[87] *CD* IV/2, 372.
[88] *CD* IV/2, 372.
[89] *CD* IV/2, 373.

those details is the Holy Spirit. Ethics in the presence of the Spirit is ethics in the presence of Christ's love. We are not dealing with a hard taskmaster but rather with One whose yoke and burden is light. This is why I refrain from arguing in advance about what details matter, precisely because there is law to which the Christian and the Christian community is always subject. That law is what renders the present Christ a moral force. The Spirit's instruction is self-effacing: its form is that of God's command. And that instruction is truly instruction inasmuch as it generates hearers. The command of the living God is to be heard. The present tense matters. The command *per se* does not exist: we only have the commanding of the living God. This, you might say, evokes a pattern of hearing in the Spirit. That just is what the community must do: hear ever anew he who commands and is command, and so obey in light of the promise. Indeed, his command is but ingredient in his love and the instrument by which the love he is claims. The Spirit is the powerful, directive presence of Christ himself: 'The Lord, the Spirit.'[90] The rule of the Spirit, his very instruction 'is the commanding of the living God'.[91] The living God has not merely commanded but still commands. His command, his will, is his Son. And his Son instructs, concretely, in the Spirit. 'The Holy Spirit who instructs the community and the individual Christian is concretely the Spirit of Jesus.'[92] The details of the moral life are, just as is the case with the 'context', subject to a 'going on'. That 'going on' is the living Jesus himself. He instructs now. His instruction takes place in the Spirit, and is to be the law of our inmost self. Specifically, the Spirit as the instruction of the living Lord Jesus awakens and summons us 'to participation in His exaltation'.[93] What is the moral life but participation in that exaltation, participation in the presence of his love? Indeed, the moral life is a life that is lived in the light of and in the presence of Another, the royal man Jesus. The Christian individual and gathered community exist by the Spirit in the light of the One by whom they live. That they can live in light of him is because they, by virtue of the Spirit, are in Him. The 'in' generates the 'in light of'. For the 'in' is not an 'in' that is inert. Rather, it has direction, indeed imparts itself as direction *in* the Holy Spirit.

---

[90] See 2 Cor. 3.18.
[91] *CD* IV/2, 373.
[92] *CD* IV/2, 373.
[93] *CD* IV/2, 373.

There is rule and law in the Christian life; there is 'basic guidance and correction' for the moral life in the Holy Spirit.[94] Guidance and correction is indeed the business of the Spirit who does not simply confront us with the command, the will of God, but rather *imparts* it to us. The conditions for concreteness in Christian ethics are thus generated outside of us; they are alien to us. Our circumstances are rather opaque, unable to be elucidated or to provide directives without the illuminating Word and the Spirit who addresses the will of God *to* us in the here and now, thereby clarifying our context. The Spirit, as the Spirit of Jesus, is the establishing Spirit, the instructing Spirit who nurtures the individual and community in Christ's love. The Christian's and the Christian community's first task is always to call upon the Spirit in order that it be established in its foundation, the living Lord Jesus Christ.

In sum, talk of the significance, the moral significance of Christ's love, is to talk of the Spirit who gives the direction of the eternal Son. Christ is not present as One whose self-witness does not have force or power, the power or force of the Spirit. The risen and ascended Christ is present: his identity is as One who is present. But his presence as a function of the love he is radically implicates; it catechizes. That is because it bears the *Creator Spiritus*, the power of our participation in his exaltation at work. Therefore, in following the Kierkegaard of *Practice in Christianity*, we have to do with a Christ who is anything but a past historical figure.

> It is indeed eighteen hundred years since Jesus Christ walked here on earth, but this is certainly not an event just like other events, which once they are over pass into history and then, as the distant past, pass into oblivion. No, his presence here on earth never becomes a thing of the past, thus does not become more and more distant.[95]

The central interest of my account is the present Christ whose person is of decisive significance because he is a person who is never without his witness, his Spirit. His identity is, furthermore, generative of witnesses, of women and men contemporary to himself. Contemporaneity is thus a commentary on the true form of Christ said to be accessible to us through faith. But it is more than that: that we can indeed 'live with Christ, in contemporaneity' is because of the Paraclete in whom God Himself is present.[96]

---

[94] *CD* IV/2, 369.

[95] Søren Kierkegaard, *Practice in Christianity*, 9, quoted in Murray Rae, *Kierkegaard and Theology* (London: T&T Clark, 2010), 69.

[96] Rae, *Kierkegaard and Theology*, 82.

The accent in my account of contemporaneity is somewhat different than that found in Kierkegaard, however. With Kierkegaard I affirm that we do not have to do with Christ merely as a past actor. That we do not have to do with him as a past actor is because, as Barth maintains, the One in whom we have been exalted *is* at work, powerfully so, such that we really may participate in him in our exaltation. It is the active character of his presence that I want to affirm. The emphasis, then, in my account is not only on following and accompanying the present Christ; more than that, it is, moving beyond Kierkegaard, on the truth that 'concrete direction…proceeds from the man Jesus'.[97] What is following then but the fresh receiving of direction? And in that receiving of Christ's mission, and of the instruction that is bound up with being sent forth in the presence of Christ's love, there is profound moral significance. That significance lies, most basically, in an ever fresh receiving of 'the commanding of the living God'.[98]

Conclusion

In this chapter I have argued that Christ's love is not something that either an individual Christian or the Christian community realize. Rather, his love is to be accepted as that which confronts us in the form of a question: 'Do you love me?' The One who asked that question of Peter is present to us as One who continues to gather, uphold and send women and men who, through the Spirit, have learnt in an all too provisional fashion to offer an affirmative answer to Him who is at work until he comes again. Christ is ministering his love unto all through those who feed his flock in his name. That it be important to give an account of Christ's presence and ongoing activity in a manner that makes recourse to his immanent identity as the eternal Son who determines himself to be this One together with the Father and Spirit is important, for the simple reason that his contemporary identity has power because it is the disclosure in time of One who always is. Moreover, he in his very person as the One who was and is, is present in the form of command. The love he is and gives, he calls forth in the power of the Spirit. Love of himself and thus the neighbour is what his ascended person generates, for to be with Christ and to be where he is in the mode of anticipation, is to reflect in the here and now his love and light which is the gift of the Spirit that all those who are in him freely receive. Thus the joy of the life of following the ascended and present Christ in the mode of the Spirit is found in being rendered ever more transparent to the love that is eternal life. Far from ignoring the details of moral existence, this love heightens our awareness of the circumscribed character of all of life. To live morally, which is to live ethically, is to be given ears that hear the commanding Christ. His person includes the command to love, specifically to love all in the presence of himself in order that human life be made more human. That is the aim of the moral life: 'What God is doing to make and to keep human life *human* in the world.'[99] Accordingly, the direction of my account is this world's radical renewal in light of the cosmic renewal that Jesus has effected through his being raised from the dead and, furthermore, is effecting through the pouring out of the Spirit to the end that all might live in accord with his life, the life that is truly life.

[99] Lehmann, *Ethics*, 99.

Chapter 5

ON WHY SCRIPTURE CONSTRUES ETHICAL REALITY

Scripture's use by God determines what it is, namely the Word of God. God uses Scripture as the chief means by which he publishes his ways and works among us such that it can be said to be *his* Word. The Word of God is a profoundly Christocentric Word, bespeaking the Son as not only its center but also as the determiner of all reality. His reality is a Scripturally construed one, and a moral one at that. Reality thus understood orients: Christ is present in the Spirit as One who indefatigably continues to do what the biblical narrative says he did. That is to say, he *is* gathering, upholding and sending witnesses forth to attest his reign of life. To affirm such an account of what Scripture is, is not to deny its humanity or its occasionality but rather to suggest that God's use of the prophetic and apostolic testimony to shape a people and form them into the image of his Son is definitive for our understanding of what Scripture is. The Father, together with his Son and the Spirit whom he receives and breathes, bespeak their reality via Scripture. Christ is present in the Spirit as One who orients, precisely because his is a reality that includes, clarifies and sets human beings on a new path of participation in the Scripturally attested work that his Father is doing together with him by the Spirit's power so as to make all things new.

USE AND BEING

Almost a generation ago George Lindbeck famously argued that 'It is the text, so to speak, which absorbs the world, rather than the world the text.'[1] Lindbeck's discussion, specifically his proposal

---

[1] Lindbeck, *Nature of Doctrine*, 118.

that religious doctrines can be viewed as a kind of 'cultural and/or linguistic framework or medium that shapes the entirety of life and thought', has elicited much discussion.[2] In this section, I will use Lindbeck's dictum as a starting point, arguing that the Bible does not only 'absorb' or 'describe' – I use these terms synonymously – reality, but also bespeaks a reality that is deeply moral or ethical, a reality that cannot be rightly understood without our being involved in its very establishment. Scripture construes a reality that is profoundly moral. The God of the Bible acts at once as the One who situates and also as One who directs; knowledge of God contextualizes and sets us on his way. If such is the case, then, what needs to complement Lindbeck's discussion is the notion that the world of the biblical text does not merely absorb or describe: it also actively shapes, by virtue of its subject matter, all of life. The text can and indeed does describe reality in expansive terms, precisely because reality – namely, the ascended and advent Christ, who speaks through it, wills to transform the world so that it might be more nearly correspondent to his covenantal purposes for it.

The driving force of my proposal all along has been Scripture: the ethical center of Christology is Scripture.[3] I say 'Scripture' and not 'ecclesiology' because priority needs to be ascribed to the utterly creative power of the written Word to create new life when appropriated to us by the Spirit. The church is a creature of this (external) Word; without this Word there would be no church. Scripture by virtue of its subject matter – Jesus Christ – attests not only what the God of Israel has done, but also what that same God is doing and will so do 'to reconcile (*apokatallaxai*) to himself all things' (Col. 1.20). The church is the firstfruits of the efficacy of God's reconciling work. This work is the 'meta-narrative', if you will, by which the church is established and with which ethics works. The meta-narrative is Christological, and therefore ethical. Scripture gives us a purchase on reality, not because of what it is *per se*, but rather because of what God does with it. God uses these texts in all of their humanity in such a way that their subject matter can be said not only to construe, but also and by virtue

---

[2] A very helpful 'complement' to Lindbeck's proposal is found in Jane Barter Moulaison's *Lord and Giver of Life: Toward a Pneumatological Complement to George Lindbeck's Theory of Doctrine* (Waterloo, ON: Wilfrid Laurier University Press, 2007).

[3] Scripture rather than 'ecclesiology' is, as Wannenwetsch argues (following Bonhoeffer), Christology's ethical center. See 'The Whole Christ and the Whole Human Being', in *Christology and Ethics*, ed. F. LeRon Shults and Brent Waters (Grand Rapids, MI: Eerdmans, 2010), 86.

of their subject matter – God's creation, maintenance and perfection of covenant fellowship with creatures – effect the real. Indeed, God proclaims and announces himself through the testimony of these texts in a way that creates a people, and so a visible correspondence to his Word and work. Stated differently, Christ's person and work is creative of a people: his presence is formative of a people who know him as One in whom their humanity is remade and being remade. His people read Scripture so as to hear and be conformed to his will to remake them in accord with what they are in him.

Scripture is, following Barth, the second form of the threefold form of the Word of God: proclaimed, written and revealed.[4] As the written Word it does not so much 'absorb' the world as set forth the real world in the most self-involving way imaginable. Scripture displays what it is that is really going on in the world: God's making of himself known. This is especially the case with respect to John's Gospel: 'Revelation, that is, God's making himself known, is precisely the theme of this Gospel.'[5] Accordingly, what Scripture is, is derivative of God's use of it as *the* instrument that he uses and so sanctifies as to address and to shape his covenant people into his people.[6]

Were I to choose a term which describes what the Gospel (and in a sense all of Scripture) is, I would invoke that of testimony. The language of testimony gives better insight into what it is that God does with these texts. God takes hold of these texts to testify to the real, to set forth the real, that which is going on in the real world, the actual world, which as such cannot be conflated with the factual.[7] Indeed, as Wolf Krötke argues, what is factual does not equal what is real.[8] In other words, reality cannot be conflated with factuality, with what is empirically verifiable. What is real is Jesus Christ, and Christ is never present without his self-witness, inclusive as it is of the apostles whose speech has become his own, whose writing faithfully attests his

---

[4] See *CD* I/1, §4.

[5] Moody Smith, *Gospel of John*, 24.

[6] The language of sanctification with regards to Scripture belongs to Webster. See *Holy Scripture*, 9.

[7] See Morse, *The Difference Heaven Makes*, 59. 'In each instance [in the two ways Barth employs saga] a poetic envisioning of divinatory imagination, a way of seeing what is going on, that allows for more actuality than factuality is said to be characteristic of saga, both in its origins and in its current hearing.'

[8] See Wolf Krötke, '*Was ist Wirklichkeit?*' (lecture, Faculty of Theology, Humboldt University, Berlin, 1 February 1995). Note that all translations of Krötke's work are my own.

ongoing gathering, upholding and sending of a people through their proclamation.

Scripture is the written Word of God because it serves God's purpose to be loved, served and praised among creatures reconciled to himself and to one another by his Son in the Spirit. To be sure, there are many genres in Holy Scripture that cannot be said to be testimony, that do not in so direct a sense as does John's Gospel attest the good news of God's rule: for example Israel's wisdom literature. But even then, Israel's wisdom literature has a specific purpose, namely that of helping Israel in an individual and corporate sense to live in a way that testifies to its status as God's dearly beloved, as God's elect set apart to declare his glory before the nations. All of Scripture serves this end, namely that of declaring God's will for his people and the form of life most appropriate to that declaration.

The primary genre with which I have worked in this essay is Gospel. To be sure, the Gospels are testimonies, written, according to the tradition, by four specific authors. And they are written, as Richard Bauckham argues, for 'all Christians', that is for a general Christian audience and not, in the case of John's Gospel, for a so-called Johannine community.[9] They are, moreover, portraits, portraits which in their very real differences from one another bespeak the activity of One whose identity and agency is eclipsed in the end by those who unto death oppose his enactment of it. The Gospel of John does not so much absorb the world as depict the 'bread of life' whose signs set forth the new creation, the present shining of the light in the darkness (John 6.35). The light that this One is and the signs he does attest that his reign of life is real. The eschatological focus is shifted by John to the present.[10] By real and present I mean to suggest, again, that John's Gospel and Scripture as a whole do not give us a window on a past world. Rather, by virtue of their subject matter – the enfleshed Word, crucified, risen and ascended in the power of the Spirit – a world is disclosed that is said to be present.

That the Gospel of John can be said to construe reality, that there is a saving address that lies at the heart of it, need not be corroborated with reference to a prior foundation outside of it. The Gospel and, by extension, the rest of Scripture, do not refer behind or beyond themselves for their referent. They are their own criteria

---

[9] See further Richard Bauckham, ed., *The Gospel for all Christians: Rethinking the Gospel Audiences* (Grand Rapids, MI: Eerdmans, 1998).

[10] See Moody Smith, *Gospel of John*, 24.

for faithfulness: 'not something behind, beneath, or in front of the text; not something that the text reveals, discloses, implies, or suggests to those with extraneous metaphysical, historical, or experiential interests'.[11] What the Gospel of John refers to, Jesus as One who overcomes the darkness thereby instituting the reign of life, is testimony that is self-authenticating in and by the power of the Holy Spirit. One need not go 'behind' the narrative or seek to establish its truthfulness by pointing to supposed verities external to it. Biblical testimony generates an account of itself, and that account and the ontology implied therein is derivative of One whose enacted identity is narratively attested and who wills to be known by this testimony; for it is *his* testimony.[12] Scripture gives us an account of what it *is* because of Another who does not will that his voice be supplanted by others, but annexes the voices of the prophets and apostles in such a way that his Word is heard through them while preserving the integrity of the voices through whom he speaks. An account of what Scripture is, is a function of the act and being of the triune God 'who uses Scripture to reshape the church into Christ's image by the Spirit's power'.[13]

REALITY OR ETHICAL REALITY: WHAT IS AT STAKE?

This essay has sought to hear the Gospel of John as depicting a history that is 'the most up-to-date'.[14] This is not to impose an intention upon John that is alien to it. To read with the grain of John's Gospel is to recognize that it is the *form* of Jesus' speech until he comes again. Because of Jesus' own words – the 'I am coming to you' of John 14.18 – we cannot read the text in a manner that assumes that its acting subject is absent, and that the world which he and his Father loves in the Spirit is not subject to their working.[15] Many works in the area of theological and Christian ethics do little exegesis; the Bible is inhabited sparingly.[16] My appropriation of John is not an addendum

---

[11] Lindbeck, *Nature of Doctrine*, 120.

[12] Webster, Introduction to Jüngel, *God's Being is in Becoming*, xx.

[13] J. Todd Billings, *The Word of God for the People of God: An Entryway into the Theological Interpretation of Scripture* (Grand Rapids, MI: Eerdmans, 2010), xiii.

[14] *CD* IV/2, 107.

[15] See John 5.17.

[16] For the distinction between Christian ethics and theological ethics, see Haddorff, *Christian Ethics as Witness*, 7: 'Christian ethics begins with a prior understanding of theological ethics, which is, at its core, an ethics of witness... In turn, if a "Christian ethics" seeks to remain theological, it too rests upon God's grace for its deliberations

to points that could very well have been made independent of it. I would not have been able to offer the account I have without this text.

Reading John in this way, so as to map the dogmatic issues at stake in the relationship of Christology and ethics, is necessary, I think, especially in light of the claim of this text (but not only this text among New Testament texts) that Jesus is present, and that as present he is working now through the Spirit in a way that aligns with his working then. This is not to take away from the 'once-and-for-all' character of his work, but rather simply to say that it lives in its being 'once-and-for-all'. The nature of his presence and of his working is a moral one demonstrative of the way in which the real establishes itself among us. By loving one another, others will know that you are mine.[17] His presence is an orienting presence which commands us to love. The way in which he orients us to himself is his written Word.

We read Scripture so as to be caught up in what is being established: the power, truth and love ingredient in the Gospel. Scripture occupies a normative status in the construal of reality because its subject matter does not attest itself as intelligible in relationship to any *a priori*. That Scripture does not refer – in the case of the Gospels – to history as the 'test of the meaning of the realistic form of the stories', reminds us that the only 'test' of these narratives' veracity is themselves. Frei's insight, derived as it is from Barth, aligns with Krötke's sense that the factual – what 'discloses itself to our visible perception' – is not always in accord with the reality rendered and conveyed by these narratives.[18] That is to say, there is not something else more real or factual by which these texts and the identity of the One enacted therein is referred.[19] Therefore we must read them in accord with their grain as that which makes claims about the way the world is: the very theater for the God of the covenant's creation, maintenance and perfection of covenant fellowship with the creature.

Scripture does not simply construe reality but *ethical* reality. That is, Scripture does not only 'absorb' the world or describe the real world. It does more in that the world it discloses, attests the presence of One who *is* making new. If we are to account for reality in terms

and actions in choosing what is ethically right. Said differently, Christian ethics as witness is a theological *reminder* about what Christian ethics *ought* to be if it remains committed to the truth of the gospel' (original emphasis).

[17] See John 13.35.

[18] See Frei, *Eclipse*, xiii; and Krötke, '*Was ist Wirklichkeit?*' (lecture).

[19] See Frei, *Eclipse*, 13.

of Christology and therefore Scripture, then we must describe reality in moral terms. To know Jesus truly as Scripturally attested is to know him as Lord, and so to follow him in his way, to be transformed. Indeed, the invitation given to the church is 'to participate in Christ's ongoing prophetic work in the world'.[20] The mission of the Son in John's Gospel is to breathe upon us his own Spirit 'which conforms us to himself'.[21] If this be so, then reality – understood to be in accord with the Son's Scriptural testimony – is not simply a matter of affirming propositional truths with respect to the way things are. Instead, reality is deeply and irrevocably *ethical.* And so, the subject matter of John's Gospel is evangelical; its *telos* is belief, participation in the life of the Son. 'But these are written so that you may come to believe that Jesus is the Messiah, the Son of God, and that through believing you may have life in his name' (John 20.31). Scripture construes reality along ethical lines because it aims at belief: love of the Son. The knowledge of the One of whom it speaks is knowledge that is acquired only deeply participatorily: 'Follow me'.

Scripture is self-involving. With Augustine, I affirm that ever increasing love of Christ is that to which Scripture would deliver us. To love Christ in this life is, for Augustine, to be, among other things, more easily delivered from evil.[22] What I think we need to be delivered from is a reading(s) of the text that resists being sanctified in the truth. An account of Scripture as construing *ethical* reality is a simple reminder that Scripture absorbs, or better, implicates. It teaches us to love the One whom we once hated. My rationale in this text for reading and expounding Scripture is to hear its testimony as that which bespeaks the ongoing presence of One who appoints, calls and commissions the Twelve and us in them to the end that he be believed and obeyed. Indeed, we, the readers and hearers, are being gathered, upheld and sent in Christ's appointing, calling and commissioning of the Twelve.[23] Talk of ethics' Christological reality and its center as being Scripture is a more formal way of describing the contemporary character of Christ's work as commensurate with our being gathered, upheld and sent forth in him by the Spirit. The reality of the text – the Son, the Father who sends and works through him, and the Paraclete who comes as the gift of the Father in the

---

[20] *CD* IV/2, 236.
[21] Tanner, *Christ the Key*, 173.
[22] See *NPNF* 7, *Augustin: Homilies on John*, 124, 5.
[23] Demson, *Barth and Frei*, 48.

Son's name – is ethical, insofar as this One cannot be said to *be* in a way that does not include our being re-made through accompanying him on his way. Indeed, to talk about what Scripture is, is to point to a person who is 'never present except as the One who indefatigably continues to gather, uphold, and send many (or all) others by including them in his appointment, calling, and commissioning of the Twelve'.[24] Scripture is testimony to his doing just that. That action of his is reality. And the reality he is, together with the Father and Spirit, is active and dynamic, making new.

THE LOCATION OF THE CHURCH

To begin ethics with Christ is not enough: ethics is to stay with Christ, to seek to be present to Christ.[25] I am not interested in only a Christological starting point for ethics: that is, Christology as only a beginning but not also the middle and end point of ethics. Ethics involves our being continually schooled by the prophets and apostles. To not only begin with but to stay with Christ, which is ethics' task, is to yield to Scripture. By yielding, the church hears and obeys Scripture's prophetic and apostolic testimony. The church is where ethical agency is nourished, insofar as it is in the church that we are baptized into Christ by the Spirit *and* nourished by the proclaimed Word and holy table. This is what I take Angus Paddison to mean when he writes: 'When considering Scripture's role in our ethical formation and discernment…we have no place to begin other than the particular reading community that is the church'.[26] In other words, the church does not occupy an accidental role when it comes to ethical formation. However, Paddison's claim, if it is to hold up to dogmatic scrutiny, needs to be underwritten and sustained by a more robust Christology. Christology and only then ecclesiology, which is to emphasize again that the church is a creature of the Word of God.

To maintain, as does Paddison (following Hauerwas and Yoder) that Scripture and the moral reasoning it engenders is dependent upon '*attention to the lived reality of Christ and the community in whose*

---

[24] Demson, *Barth and Frei*, 48.

[25] My main criticism of David Haddorff's *Christian Ethics as Witness* is that the emphasis throughout his text is on Christ as ethics' starting point, which is of course true. But he does not follow through on what is also true, for Barth anyhow: Christ is the one whose gift of freedom in the Spirit maintains and perfects ethics.

[26] Angus Paddison, *Scripture: A Very Theological Proposal* (London: T&T Clark, 2009), 33.

life it ['the lived reality of Christ'] is embedded' elides two important Christological points.[27] First, the notion of embeddedness overlooks, I think, the fragility and profound provisionality of the church's attention to Christ: it is the church that needs, even more than the 'world', to actually *hear* the Gospel. Hence, we need to think about the relationship between Scripture and ethics first and foremost in relation to the necessity of hearing Christ. Accordingly, 'embedding' language detracts from Christ's sovereignty over the community: his freedom to speak over and against it through his Word as a function of his being for it. Put again, claims about the church in relation to Christ and ethics ought to be rightly situated in the light of a Christ whose presence includes law: 'Do not sin again' (John 8.11).

Second, we hear Scripture in the church, to be sure. But to say that 'the church is the school where we learn to be part of God's story' seems to shortchange the agency of the ascended Christ who creates through prophetic and apostolic testimony the Christian community. The community he creates does not so much 'embody' him. It is, rather, a community continually gathered to him, and upheld and sent by him into the world, in the Spirit's power and in accord with the promise.[28]

In the end, I remain more cautious than Paddison with respect to the dogmatic location of the church. I agree that Scripture can never, as he avers, be isolated '*from its relationship to Christ and its location within the church*'.[29] That said, I am not as convinced that Scripture's 'moral significance', to use Hauerwas's term, comes down to 'what kind of community the church must be to make the narrative of scripture central to its life'.[30] I think that Scripture's moral significance lies more in the notion that God uses it to attest reality, and that reality it bespeaks *is* ethical: Christ and the Spirit and us in them. To be sure, I do not think that Paddison would for a moment disagree with me. It is simply that the emphasis I offer in my account does shift – albeit with subtlety – the focus onto the present Christ whose relentless and unceasing activity is narrated for us in his Word in a way that makes it impossible to talk about that Christ without one's

---

[27] Paddison, *Scripture*, 45, original emphasis.

[28] Paddison, *Scripture*, 44.

[29] Paddison, *Scripture*, 45, original emphasis.

[30] Stanley Hauerwas, *Community of Character: Toward a Constructive Social Ethic*, 2nd ed. (Notre Dame, IN: Notre Dame University Press, 2008), 56–7, quoted in Paddison, *Scripture*, 68.

dispositions being profoundly reoriented within the context of his body over which he remains Lord.

ON WHY SCRIPTURE CANNOT BE APPLIED

Isaac Dorner writes that 'Christ *is* what he teaches'.[31] To use the terms of this essay, Christ is the form of the power, truth and love he teaches. Christ is the new life he creates in us through the Spirit. Christ gives us the power to live with, to accompany him on his way. But again, we are in him with whom we (should) live – albeit in the mode of promise. One of the implications of describing Scriptural reality in dynamic and expansive terms is that it obviates talk of its needing to be applied. That is to say, talk of applying suggests that Scripture might very well tell us how things are, but it is nonetheless we who are responsible for bringing what it discloses into being, for incarnating it, making it relevant, etc. To talk about the Gospel of John as providing an account of the truth which we then need to apply to the 'real world' misconstrues the nature of moral or ethical reality. Reality understood Christologically is not well served by the notion of application as it suggests that we are the center to which all else must refer. Indeed, the language of application trades upon an account of an inert subject matter and an overinflated sense of the self and/or community.

If we turn for a moment to John 21, we are reminded once more that the seven (and we in them) are quite adept at absconding from the Lord. Individual Christians and the gathered community are well versed in returning to what they were: creatures dead in trespasses and sins. That Jesus 'showed (*ephanerōsen*) himself' to them in such a way as to restore them to what they are, namely his disciples, helps us see why referring to Scripture as needing application is problematic. Scripture is first and foremost an address that needs to be heard as the discourse of One who unceasingly speaks or shows himself through its pages. Its authority does not lie in its ability to speak to our situations, or arise to the degree to which it resonates with us, its hearers. Biblical commands such as the particular command spoken to Peter – 'Follow me' – are not commands that he or we as those addressed in Jesus' address to Peter need apply. We need, rather, to hear so as to obey.

The Bible's moral authority is inextricably bound up with the present and ministering Christ. Talk of the Bible's authority – partic-

---

[31] I. A. Dorner, *System of Christian Ethics* (Edinburgh: T&T Clark, 1906), 347.

ularly its commands – is derivative of an authoritative presence: namely Christ present as the appointing, calling and commissioning Word, and so the upholding, gathering and sending Word. He in his person is command: Christ is God's command, what God wills. If Christ's person is what he teaches and commands, description *and* prescription, past and present, then O'Donovan's sense that the most mysterious question for moral reasoning: 'What does the situation that I am facing mean?' is not quite right. I say not quite right because the location of the 'I' and the 'situation' is mapped, for O'Donovan, in a way that shortchanges the growth proper to Christ's 'objective achievement'.[32] Hence, there is no longer an 'I' or a 'situation' at all independent of the Christ who *shows* himself. The meaning of the situation and what we are to do in relationship to it can only be mapped in relation to Christ's relentless self-presentation in Word and Spirit. Faith is a matter of perceiving, then, of acting in agreement with he who *is* there and at work: the 'incessant redeemer'.[33] The present tense, the self-giving of the Son in the Spirit, is crucial to acknowledge if the context be properly elucidated. It means that the more important question becomes, I think, 'What does the "situation" ask of me in light of Christ's very definite presence and concrete activity in relationship to it?'

To suggest that the command to Peter – 'Follow me' – 'applies' to me or to us does not quite rightly account, moreover, for how we are addressed by the command spoken to Peter, or by the commands spoken by Jesus in John's Gospel. Indeed, the command is not given to us as either a 'moral rule' or 'public law'.[34] I am unsure as to how a command spoken to Peter which assumes a universal horizon, which thereby transcends its occasionality, functions as a 'moral rule'. We are, rather, called to obey a person whose word is transparent to the working of the One whom he calls 'Father'. The Bible construes moral reality – reality as moral, as profoundly invested in conforming us to itself – because it is, as a whole, a function of the promise: 'You will be my people' (Ezek. 37.29). The Bible's authority is not intrinsic to itself but rather to him who claims. What God wills for

---

[32] P. T. Forsyth, *The Person and Place of Christ* (London: Independent Press, 1948), 329.

[33] Forsyth, *Person and Place*, 340.

[34] These are, for Oliver O'Donovan, the 'two types of general moral instruction, as they appear in the Bible'. O'Donovan, 'The Moral Authority of Scripture', in *Scripture's Doctrine and Theology's Bible*, ed. Markus Bockmuehl and Alan J. Torrance (Grand Rapids, MI: Baker Academic, 2008), 173.

us is Christ. What Christ wills to do with us is to include (all) others in his commissioning of the Twelve. His commission to 'follow' thus has authority because it is *his*. It is the very command ingredient in his person. Hence the language of 'hermeneutical distance', and thus 'a gap between reader and the text, a gap that understanding has to overcome', is relativized by the subject matter of the text.[35] Accordingly, what is at issue is not so much one of biblical meaning, that is 'how does it affect us?' Rather, it is a matter of Christ who overcomes the distance, ordering us to himself via his Word.[36]

The command spoken to Peter is not only a word that affects us. It *is* the Word of the Lord to us. There is, of course, a gap between the late modern world and first-century Palestine. However, Christ's teaching about his coming again, his abiding in those who obey him, is contemporary because for him there is no gap. He lives. He continues to commission disciples for the ministry of feeding through words spoken two millennia ago; for those words of Jesus are his. They effect a transformative encounter. Indeed, he has annexed the words of the prophets and apostles in such a way that they are his, and so 'understanding' need not do work that he by his Spirit can only properly do. 'Presence' trumps the language of 'meaning' and 'affecting' because it bespeaks Christ as present in a very definite sense, as One including us in his activity in relation to the Twelve. Reality, in short, cannot be applied. It can only be heard and so be obeyed.

THE CHURCH AND THE PRESENCE OF CHRIST

The primary locus of Christ's presence is not the church so much as the (written) Word. This is not to suggest an indifferent stance toward the church, but rather to ascribe priority to the written Word when talking about the character of Christ's presence. What is at stake in this can be seen by referring to Bernd Wannenwetsch's careful reading of Bonhoeffer's Christology lectures of 1933. Commenting on them, Wannenwetsch writes: 'Personal presence, in turn, is articulated [for Bonhoeffer] in temporal, spatial, and relational terms, which again reinforces the claim of the sole accessibility of Christ in and as his body, the church.'[37] If I could inflect the statement somewhat

---

[35] O' Donovan, 'Moral Authority', in *Scripture's Doctrine*, 173.

[36] O' Donovan, 'Moral Authority', in *Scripture's Doctrine*, 174.

[37] Wannenwetsch, 'The Whole Christ and the Whole Human Being', in *Christology*

differently, I would say: personal presence might be better articulated in temporal (here and now), active (dynamic), and expansive (including us in itself) terms, which again reinforces the claim that the primary accessibility of Christ is in and through his written Word, which generates hearers who in turn become the earthly-historical form of his existence. When heard in faith, the Gospel of Christ renders us transparent to Christ and so creates disciples, followers, the church.

Ultimately, I want to think of Christ's presence under the 'impression' of his ministry, and so view his resurrection and ascension as the basis of his ministry's contemporaneity.[38] Christ is present as One who gathers, upholds and sends (many or all). This is why Christology's ethical center is Scripture. The church as his body is the response to his written Word, his proclamation of himself which is the chief form of his ministering presence. And so, Christ's presence in the world is first and foremost a ministering presence: Scripture gives us a Christ who in the Spirit is always working. Hence when it comes to statements like 'the church exists as Christ's presence in the world by virtue of its sacramentality', I would rather suggest that the church's existence as a community of Word and Sacrament is as much because of Christ's ministry.[39] The church's sacraments effectively signify his continual presence in the mode of promise until he comes again.

The issue really is the 'as': that is, whether it is appropriate to speak of Christ existing *as* community. Christ exists, first, as prophet, priest and king, proclaiming his mediatorial rule through the written Word as sealed by the sacraments. His proclamation is never without effect, and so the church exists as the firstfruits of his ministering presence. Christ's form (*gestalt*) within space and time *is* his ministry. Concreteness in ethics is achieved by Christ's ongoing activity as living minister. I do not think that focus on his ministry is one-sided precisely because his ministry is also that of a priest and king. The

and Ethics, 81. Note that the 'later' Bonhoeffer posits more of a disjuncture between Christ and the church. Indeed, by the time he writes his *Ethics* manuscripts the focus is more on the 'form' of Christ in the world as giving rise to a church that can only claim to be the church when it exists for others in vicarious responsible action.

[38] Wannenwetsch somewhat differently, following Bonhoeffer, thinks of Christ's presence 'under the impression of his resurrection and ascension'. See Wannenwetsch, 'The Whole Christ and the Whole Human Being', in *Christology and Ethics*, 82.

[39] Wannenwetsch, 'The Whole Christ and the Whole Human Being', in *Christology and Ethics*, 86.

ministry of Christ refers to his ministry as 'prophet, priest, and king'. The account of the moral life that his ministry engenders is thus deeply tied to Scripture as the testimony to what his life wills to achieve among us: the continual gathering, upholding and sending of all others in his name. As priest, he continues to mediate between his Father and the world, and as king he rules in accord with his Father's will to forgive and restore. The moral life is indeed 'the active answer to Christ', the Christ who renders through his Spirit women and men in agreement with himself in the context of his body the church.[40] And so, Christ's ministry in the world is that of achieving *moral* knowledge: the obedience of faith. Moral or ethical knowledge arises first and foremost in relation to Scripture, to hearing it as the primary form in which Christ comes and speaks to us. Scripture construes reality as ethical, thereby raising up and turning humankind in such a way that it might be where he is and love others in his name and so love until he comes again.[41]

The relationship between Christ and ethics is best described from within Scripture, and thus from within Christ's ministry which is One of gathering into his body, upholding through the sacramental life of his body, and sending as reflection of the utterly creative and expansive power of his ministry in Word and Spirit. I remain unconvinced, then, that the task of the church is one of 'performance' of Christ's Lordship.[42] Rather, the church's joy is to be present to what Christ wills. One of the church's primary acts – its confession of sin and its being daily subject to repentance in accord with its baptism – attests that it does not 'perform' Christ at all well. This is not so because Christ performs himself poorly. Rather, his performance is definite, and people as a consequence are taken up into it, albeit often all too provisionally. Christ keeps on performing a certain activity, namely that of making disciples and of commissioning men and women to love him and so feed the sheep in his name. His performance evokes a human echo; he never wills to be present without his apostles and those whom he calls through them. So in a kind of secondary sense, the church does perform Christ;

[40] Wannenwetsch, 'The Whole Christ and the Whole Human Being', in *Christology and Ethics*, 94.

[41] A 'Christologically saturated ethic' asks: 'Does this or that instance of human conduct "belong" here – in the presence of Christ, *Christus praesens, totus Christus, Christus pro nobis*?' See Wannenwetsch, 'The Whole Christ and the Whole Human Being', in *Christology and Ethics*, 97.

[42] See Paddison, *Scripture*, 37.

but such performance is, again, through the power of Christ himself in Word and Spirit. His performance of himself is definite, for it is grounded in his coming to be 'what he always vitally was'.[43] The issue with 'performance' language is, quite simply, that it detracts from his glory as mediator. He shines with unutterable brightness. The necessary corollary of his shining is a people who attest in word and deed his shining.

Scripture is a clear and perspicuous Word: *Klarheit* is ingredient in it because of the promise of the Spirit: 'He will guide you into all the truth (*alētheias*)' (John 16.13). Therefore, we do not strive to make Scripture's message concrete, but rather submit to the conditions it gives whereby its concreteness is fulfilled: *his* ministry as ongoing 'until the full number of the Gentiles has come in' (Rom. 11.25). The only way in which Scripture's moral significance is recognized is for the church to be present to the Lord through Word and Spirit, the Lord whose self-disclosure is morally significant: 'Do you love me?'[44] Said differently, 'Here [in Scripture] something has been said and we want to hear.'[45] That is what the church must do. Jesus Christ has been said and in the Spirit is being said. The church's primary task is not to be a certain kind of community in order that it may 'make the narrative of scripture central for its life'.[46] Instead, the church's task is to conform truly to its inner being – Jesus Christ. When heard in faith, the narrative of Scripture makes the church into its true self: Christ's body. A church 'in the ruins' can only begin at the beginning with what 'has been said', which is what, by the Spirit, is being said.[47] These narratives render the real, and the real as it communicates itself 'orients men's dispositions'.[48]

The written Word of God cannot but do otherwise because attached to it is the promise that it will 'not return to me empty' (Isa. 55.11). Questions of meaning, it seems, are really better construed as being questions of orientation or of order. 'Meaning is a function of knowing reality', and reality orients.[49] To be sure, late modernity

---

[43] Forsyth, *Person and Place*, 338.

[44] Hauerwas, *Community of Character*, 56, quoted in Paddison, *Scripture*, 63.

[45] Karl Barth, *God in Action: Theological Addresses*, trans. E. G. Homrighausen and Karl J. Ernst (Edinburgh: T&T Clark, 1937), 108.

[46] Hauerwas, *Community of Character*, 56, quoted in Paddison, *Scripture*, 63.

[47] That wording is taken from Rusty Reno's book entitled *In the Ruins of the Church: Sustaining Faith in an Age of Diminished Christianity* (Grand Rapids, MI: Brazos, 2002).

[48] Frei, *Eclipse*, 156.

[49] Frei, *Eclipse*, 101.

'renders faith in God impossible'.[50] But Scripture, when illumined by the Spirit, bespeaks a determination and determining reality: 'The event of God and the faith which this event creates cannot be excluded from the understanding of reality.'[51] Although since Kant, reality refers to that 'which in time and space is perceivable, if not material', the Bible, in particular John's Gospel, would have us see otherwise.[52] Says Krötke, 'To reality belongs the assertion of reality itself.'[53] In other words, Christ is self-promoting: he asserts himself in such a way that we are taken up through the Spirit into his life. That is Jesus Christ's plerosis or self-fulfillment. He wills to fulfill himself in us. In this regard, Forsyth writes, 'Only one who incarnated God's holiest will as His Son alone did could produce and establish in men for ever the due response to that will – the response of their whole and holy selves.'[54] Through the Spirit, it is Jesus who makes disciples by including them in the commission given to the Twelve; it is he who in the Spirit creates hearers of his Scripturally spoken Word.

CONCLUSION

Christ is our contemporary. To become contemporary with him is to accompany him on his way. To follow him, as Murray Rae reminds us, involves a cost, 'the cost involved in venturing out beyond the security of objective certainties, worldly possessions, finite aspirations and society's approval'.[55] The Christ to be followed is the Christ of Holy Scripture. Scripture attests a Christ who is not a prisoner of his historical context. The reading of John offered in this essay assumes that the only solid basis from which to understand the Gospel is not so much 'a study of the text of the Fourth Gospel itself and an effort to set it in its historical context', but rather a study of the text as the chief means by which the One who enacts his identity therein is known.[56] The Gospel need not be set in its historical context so much as in its own Christological context. The Christ who gives himself to the world as life and light is the One who situates us via this text (John's Gospel) and other Scriptural texts. That is why his reality

---

[50] Krötke, '*Was ist Wirklichkeit?*' (lecture).
[51] Krötke, '*Was ist Wirklichkeit?*' (lecture).
[52] Krötke, '*Was ist Wirklichkeit?*' (lecture).
[53] Krötke, '*Was ist Wirklichkeit?*' (lecture).
[54] Forsyth, *Person and Place*, 327.
[55] Rae, *Kierkegaard and Theology*, 180.
[56] Moody Smith, *Gospel of John*, 7.

is a moral one, and why Scripture can be said to construe reality as moral. The Christ whom it narrates is One who is never present except as One in whom all of fallen human essence participates. He is the second Adam, and so human beings, whether they believe it to be true or not, participate in his recapitulation, his reconstitution of the human race through his life, cross and resurrection in fidelity to the promises made to his people Israel. The only context in which the text of the Fourth Gospel would set us is Christ. To be sure, he is a first-century Palestinian Jew; but as this Jew he lives for all.

The key to understanding Jesus Christ is his person. Scripture construes him as a deeply moral figure, One whose self-presentation is such that 'grace might also exercise dominion through justification (*dikaiosunēs*) leading to eternal life' (Rom. 5.21). This One just is 'righteousness and sanctification and redemption' (1 Cor. 1.30) or, to use Johannine language, ' "the resurrection and the life" ' (John 10.30). As such, the writings which attest him construe as a reality that implicates so as to make new. If this book be of any value, it will have drawn attention to the present tense of the biblical witness concerning this One. In him we participate, not only in terms of his person and all the benefits therein, but also in his work, his ministry. Until he comes again, he and the One whom he calls Father are at work, calling us in the power of the Spirit to be transparent to that work, and so to 'love one another. By this everyone will know that you are my disciples, if you have love for one another' (John 13.35).

BIBLIOGRAPHY

Anderson, Ray S. *On Being Human: Essays in Theological Anthropology.* Pasadena, CA: Fuller Seminary Press, 1982.

Barth, Karl. *The Word of God and the Word of Man.* Trans. Douglas Horton. Cleveland, OH: Pilgrim Press, 1928.

— *God in Action: Theological Addresses.* Trans. E. G. Homrighausen and Karl J. Ernst. Edinburgh: T&T Clark, 1937.

— *Church Dogmatics.* Ed. T. F. Torrance and G. W. Bromiley. 14 vols. Edinburgh: T&T Clark, 1936–77.

— *Ethics.* Trans. Geoffrey W. Bromiley. Edinburgh: T&T Clark, 1978.

— *The Knowledge of God and The Service of God According to the Teaching of the Reformation: Recalling the Scottish Confession of 1560.* Trans. J. L. M. Haire and Ian Henderson. Eugene, OR: Wipf and Stock, 2005.

Bauckham, Richard. *The Theology of the Book of Revelation.* Cambridge: Cambridge University Press, 1993.

Bauckham, Richard, ed. *The Gospel for all Christians: Rethinking the Gospel Audiences.* Grand Rapids, MI: Eerdmans, 1998.

Bavinck, Herman. *Reformed Dogmatics.* Trans. John Vriend. Vol. 2, *God and Creation.* Grand Rapids, MI: Baker Academic, 2004.

Billings, J. Todd. *The Word of God for the People of God: An Entryway into the Theological Interpretation of Scripture.* Grand Rapids, MI: Eerdmans, 2010.

Bird, Michael F., and Preston M. Sprinkle, eds. *The Faith of Christ: Exegetical, Biblical, and Theological.* Peabody, MA: Hendrickson, 2010.

Bonhoeffer, Dietrich. 'Protestantism without Reformation'. Trans. Edwin W. Robertson & John Bowden, in *No Rusty Swords: Letters, Lectures and Notes, 1928–1936,* 92–93 London: Collins, 1965.

— *Christ the Center.* Trans. Edwin H. Robertson. San Francisco: HarperCollins, 1978.

— *Meditating on the Word.* Ed. and trans. David McI. Gracie. Cambridge, MA: Cowley, 1986.

— *Dietrich Bonhoeffer Works*. Ed. Wayne Whitson Floyd Jr. 16 vols. Minneapolis: Fortress Press, 1996–2011.

Borg, Marcus J., and N. T. Wright. *The Meaning of Jesus: Two Visions*. New York: HarperCollins, 1999.

Brown, Raymond E. *The Gospel According to John*. 2 vols. Anchor Bible 29–29A. Garden City, NY: Doubleday, 1970.

Calvin, John. *Calvin's New Testament Commentaries*. Part 2, *The Gospel According to St. John*. Grand Rapids, MI: Eerdmans, 1959.

— *Institutes of the Christian Religion*. Ed. John T. McNeill. Philadelphia: Westminster Press, 1965.

Cunningham, David S. *Christian Ethics: The End of the Law*. London: Routledge, 2008.

Dalferth, Ingolf U. 'God, Time, and Orientation: "Presence" and "Absence" in Religious and Everyday Discourse', in *The Presence and Absence of God: Claremont Studies in the Philosophy of Religion Conference 2008*, ed. Ingolf U. Dalferth, 1–20. Tübingen: Mohr Siebeck, 2009.

Demson, David E. *Karl Barth and Hans Frei: Different Ways of Reading Scripture*. Grand Rapids, MI: Eerdmans, 1997.

Dodd, C. H. *The Interpretation of the Fourth Gospel*. Cambridge: Cambridge University Press, 1970.

Dorner, I. A. *System of Christian Ethics*. Edinburgh: T&T Clark, 1906.

Farrow, Douglas. 'Karl Barth on the Ascension: An Appreciation and Critique', *International Journal of Systematic Theology* 12.2 (2000): 127–50.

Forsyth, P. T. *The Person and Place of Christ*. London: Independent Press, 1948.

Frei, Hans W. *The Eclipse of Biblical Narrative*. New Haven, CT: Yale University Press, 1974.

— *The Identity of Jesus Christ: With Theological Reflections on the Accounts of Jesus' Death and Resurrection*. Eugene, OR: Wipf and Stock, 1997.

Haddorff, David. *Christian Ethics as Witness: Barth's Ethics for a World at Risk*. Eugene, OR: Cascade, 2010.

Hauerwas, Stanley. *Community of Character: Toward a Constructive Social Ethic*. 2nd ed. Notre Dame, IN: Notre Dame University Press, 2008.

— *Hannah's Child: A Theological Memoir*. Grand Rapids, MI: Eerdmans, 2010.

Healy, Nicholas M. 'Misplaced Concreteness? Practices and the New Ecclesiology', *International Journal of Systematic Theology* 5 (Fall 2003): 287–308.

Heppe, Heinrich. *Reformed Dogmatics: Set out and Illustrated from the Sources*. London: George Allen & Unwin, 1950.

Holmes, Christopher R. J. 'God's Attributes as God's Clarities: Wolf Krötke's Doctrine of the Divine Attributes', *International Journal of Systematic Theology* 10 (January 2008): 54–72.

— 'Barth on the Economy: In Dialogue with Kathryn Tanner', in *Commanding Grace: Studies in Karl Barth's Ethics*, ed. Daniel L. Migliore, 198–215. Grand Rapids, MI: Eerdmans, 2010.

— ' "The Indivisible Whole of God's Reality": On the Agency of Jesus in Bonhoeffer's *Ethics*', *International Journal of Systematic Theology* 12 (July 2010): 283–301.

— ' "A Specific Form of Relationship": On the Dogmatic Implications of Barth's Account of Election and Commandment for his Theological Ethics', in *Trinity and Election in Contemporary Theology*, ed. Michael Dempsey, 188–200. Grand Rapids, MI: Eerdmans, 2011.

Hoskyns, E. C. 'The Christ of the Synoptic Gospels', in *Essays Catholic and Critical*, ed. Edward Gordon Selwyn, 151–78. London: SPCK, 1926.

— *The Fourth Gospel*. 2 vols. London: Faber and Faber, 1940.

Jenson, Robert W. *Systematic Theology*. Vol. 1, *The Triune God*. New York: Oxford University Press, 1997.

Jüngel, Eberhard. *God's Being is in Becoming: The Trinitarian Being of God in the Theology of Karl Barth*. Trans. John Webster. Grand Rapids, MI: Eerdmans, 2001.

Kierkegaard, Søren. *Søren Kierkegaard's Journals and Papers*. Bloomington, IN: Indiana University Press, 1967–78.

— *Practice in Christianity*. Princeton, NJ: Princeton University Press, 1991.

Klemm, David E., and William Schweiker. *Religion and the Human Future: An Essay on Theological Humanism*. Malden, MA: Blackwell, 2008.

Krötke, Wolf. '*Was ist Wirklichkeit?*' Lecture presented at the Faculty of Theology, Humboldt University, Berlin, 1 February 1995.

— *Gottes Klarheiten: Eine Neuinterpretation der Lehre von Gottes 'Eigenschaften'*. Tübingen: Mohr Siebeck, 2001.

Lehmann, Paul L. *Ethics in a Christian Context*. Louisville, KY: Westminster John Knox, 2006.

Lessing, Gotthold. *Lessing's Theological Writings*. Trans. Henry Chadwick. London: A&C Black, 1956.

Lindbeck, George A. *The Nature of Doctrine: Religion and Theology in a Postliberal Age*. Philadelphia: Westminster Press, 1984.

Lukes, Steven. *Power: A Radical View*, 2nd ed. Basingstoke: Palgrave Macmillan, 2005.

Migliore, Daniel L. *The Power of God and the Gods of Power*. Louisville, KY: Westminster John Knox, 2008.

Moody Smith, D. *The Theology of the Gospel of John*. Cambridge: Cambridge University Press, 1995.

Morse, Christopher. *The Difference Heaven Makes: Rehearing the Gospel as News*. London: T&T Clark, 2010.

Moulaison, Jane Barter. *Lord and Giver of Life: Toward a Pneumatological Complement to George Lindbeck's Theory of Doctrine*. Waterloo, ON: Wilfrid Laurier University Press, 2007.

Newbigin, Lesslie. *The Light Has Come: An Exposition of the Fourth Gospel*. Grand Rapids, MI: Eerdmans, 1982.

Niebuhr, Reinhold. *An Interpretation of Christian Ethics*, 3rd ed. London: SCM, 1941.

O'Donovan, Oliver. *Resurrection and Moral Order: An Outline for Evangelical Ethics*. Grand Rapids, MI: Eerdmans, 1986.

— 'The Moral Authority of Scripture', in *Scripture's Doctrine and Theology's Bible*, ed. Markus Bockmuehl and Alan J. Torrance, 165–76. Grand Rapids, MI: Baker Academic, 2008.

Paddison, Angus. *Scripture: A Very Theological Proposal*. London: T&T Clark, 2009.

Pelikan, Jaroslav. *The Christian Tradition: A History of the Development of Doctrine*. Vol. 1, *The Emergence of the Catholic Tradition (100–600)*. Chicago: University of Chicago Press, 1971.

Rae, Murray. *Kierkegaard and Theology*. London: T&T Clark, 2010.

Reno, Rusty. *In the Ruins of the Church: Sustaining Faith in an Age of Diminished Christianity*. Grand Rapids, MI: Brazos, 2002.

Russell, Norman. *Commentary on John's Gospel*. In *Cyril of Alexandria*, 96–129. London: Routledge, 2000.

Rutledge, Fleming. *Not Ashamed of the Gospel: Sermons from Paul's Letter to the Romans*. Grand Rapids, MI: Eerdmans, 2007.

Schaff, Philip, ed. *St. Augustin: Homilies on the Gospel of John; Homilies on the First Epistle of John; Soliloquies*. In Vol. 7 of *The Nicene and Post-Nicene Fathers of the Christian Church*. 1st series. Ed. Philip Schaff. 1886–1889. 14 vols. Repr. Edinburgh: T&T Clark, 1986.

Schweiker, William. *Responsibility and Christian Ethics*. Cambridge: Cambridge University Press, 1995.

Stubbs, David. 'Returning to the Wilderness', unpublished manuscript, July 2010.

Sykes, Stephen. *Power and Christian Theology*. London: T&T Clark, 2006.

Tanner, Kathryn. *Christ the Key.* Cambridge: Cambridge University Press, 2010.

Taylor, Charles. *A Secular Age.* Cambridge, MA: Belknap Press of Harvard University Press, 2007.

Torrance, Thomas F. *The Mediation of Christ.* Rev. ed. Colorado Springs, CO: Helmers & Howard, 1992.

— *Incarnation: The Person and Life of Christ.* Ed. Robert T. Walker. Downers Grove, IL: IVP Academic, 2008.

— *Atonement: The Person and Work of Christ.* Ed. Robert T. Walker. Downers Grove, IL: IVP Academic, 2009.

Wannenwetsch, Bernd. *Political Worship: Ethics for Christian Citizens.* Trans. Margaret Kohl. Oxford: Oxford University Press, 2004.

— 'The Whole Christ and the Whole Human Being', in *Christology and Ethics,* ed. F. LeRon Shults and Brent Waters. Grand Rapids, MI: Eerdmans, 2010.

Ward, Graham. *The Politics of Discipleship: Becoming Postmaterial Citizens.* Grand Rapids, MI: Baker Academic, 2009.

Webster, John. *Word and Church: Essays in Dogmatics I.* Edinburgh: T&T Clark, 2001.

— *Holy Scripture: A Dogmatic Sketch.* Cambridge: Cambridge University Press, 2003.

— Review of *Wie Geschöfe Leben: Some Dogmatic Reflections,* by Hans Ulrich. *Studies in Christian Ethics* 20.2 (2007): 273–85.

— 'Resurrection and Scripture', in *Christology and Scripture: Interdisciplinary Perspectives,* ed. Andrew T. Lincoln and Angus Paddison 138–57. London: T&T Clark, 2008.

— ' "Where Christ is": Christology and Ethics', in *Christology and Ethics,* ed. F. LeRon Shults and Brent Waters, 32–55, Grand Rapids, MI: Eerdmans, 2010.

Wells, Samuel. *God's Companions: Reimagining Christian Ethics.* Malden, MA: Blackwell, 2006.

Wells, Samuel, and Ben Quash. *Introducing Christian Ethics.* Malden, MA: Wiley-Blackwell, 2010.

Ziegler, Philip G. ' "Not to Abolish but to Fulfill": The Person of the Preacher and the Sermon on the Mount', *Studies in Christian Ethics* 22.3 (2009): 275–89.

— 'Promeity in the Christologies of Bonhoeffer and Kierkegaard', Paper presented at the Annual Meeting of the American Academy of Religion, Atlanta, GA, October, 2010.

INDEX OF BIBLICAL REFERENCES

159

INDEX OF NAMES AND SUBJECTS